WEST CORK

A PLACE APART

JO KERRIGAN

Jo grew up amid the wild beauties of West Cork; after a distinguished academic and journalistic career in the UK, she returned to her roots and now writes regularly for the *Irish Examiner* and *Evening Echo*, as well as international magazines.

RICHARD MILLS

Richard was born in Provence and moved to West Cork at the age of sixteen. He combines a career of press photographer with the *Irish Examiner* and *Evening Echo*, with that of keen wildlife photographer, winning many international awards, creating a popular book on Irish birdlife, and seeing his images published across the world.

WEST CORK
A PLACE APART

JO KERRIGAN AND RICHARD MILLS

THE O'BRIEN PRESS
DUBLIN

First published 2010 by The O'Brien Press Ltd,
12 Terenure Road East, Rathgar, Dublin 6, Ireland.
Tel: +353 1 4923333; Fax: +353 1 4922777
E-mail: books@obrien.ie; Website: www.obrien.ie

ISBN: 978-1-84717-166-5

Printed in China by Kwong Fat Offset Printing Co. Ltd.
The paper used in this book is produced using pulp from managed forests.

Cover, front: Crookhaven and Streek Head.
Cover, back: Sunrise, the Gearagh.
Page 1: Greater willow herb in a bluebell wood.
Pages 2-3: Dunbeacon Castle, Dunmanus Bay.
Pages 4-5: Montbretia.
Pages 6-7: Dursey Island.

A place to create golden memories, experience the challenge of boat, sea and spray. Where ancient sites keep their own silent counsel, and small villages bustle with life. A place to wander by quiet streams, explore flower-filled laneways. Where the light is ever changing, and every corner turned brings another secret yet to be discovered.
West Cork, a place of dreams.

CONTENTS

CHAPTER I

TRUE WEST

GEARAGH, GAELTACHT, GOUGANE

Winding green lanes and chuckling streams, mysterious lake dwellings and secret valleys, drowned forests and misty mountains: this, surely, is the region JRR Tolkien had in mind when he created Middle Earth.

There is something of a tendency among travel writers to equate West Cork with its coastline alone. Understandably perhaps, since few can resist that enchantingly irregular landscape, all headlands and inlets, blue sea and splendid beaches. However, it's time to put the record straight. The inland region, stretching due west from Cork city along the valley of the river Lee, surely has first call on the title, and although doubtless not all would agree, that lovely area is given the rightful place of honour in opening this book. The rest of West Cork will just have to wait its turn.

Overall, this is a landscape effortlessly dominated by the Lee, as well as that waterway's many enthusiastic tributaries like the Bride, the Dripsey, the Sullane, which over the centuries have carved out valleys and cut meandering routes through the rich green countryside as they rush eagerly to swell the strength of the parent river. You are never far away from running water here. A complex network of rivers and streams, quiet pools where tiny fish glimmer above sunlit gravel, open reaches with richly embroidered coverlets of waterweed, bouncy little rapids where you might glimpse the vivid blue flash of a kingfisher – finally all come together to flow through Cork city as one. (And even then, the Lee can't quite make up its mind to settle in a single route, but, as Edmund Spenser famously observed in *The Faerie Queene*, 'encloseth Corke with his divided flood.')

Heading west, though, you're leaving behind the powerful and confident river

upon which the city was founded, and tracing its route westward to its source in the mountains of Gougane Barra. Deciding which road to follow might be a problem. One of the most engaging things about wandering westward out of Cork is being able to choose a different road, an alternative route, almost any day of the week, depending on your humour, the time you have to spare, and the weather that's in it. Nor is it possible to create a neat sequential itinerary, taking you smoothly from A through B and C to D. Exploring this riverine region should be viewed more like a series of individual excursions, a leap this way and then that, taking a side road on a whim, changing plans entirely as you are distracted by a mysterious boreen, an enigmatic grey stone on a hillside, a faded fingerpost leading to somewhere not shown on any map.

Dripsey to Coachford and Carrigadrohid

Even leaving the city itself you have the choice between the north and the south roads bordering the Lee – the narrower R618 meandering through Dripsey, Coachford and Carrigadrohid, or the main N22 which bypasses the suburbs and

Below: Carrignamuck Castle stands on a high rock above the Dripsey river. **Opposite top:** Carrigadrohid Castle is unusual in that it is sited right in the middle of the river, controlling the bridge which crosses at this point. **Opposite below:** Crosses, etched blackly against the evening sky, at medieval Kilcrea Abbey.

heads swiftly for Macroom. Since most traffic takes the faster southern road, you could have the quieter northern route almost to yourself. Cross Inniscarra bridge by the venerable inn where fishermen have gathered for generations to swap tales and compare catches, and turn down to see ruined St Senan's Abbey drowsing by the riverside before continuing to Dripsey, self-proclaimed home of the shortest St Patrick's Day of the twentieth century. For several years on 17 March enthusiastic participants would gather in one of the village's two pubs and then march with great pomp and ceremony to the other, a distance of some twenty-five yards. 'Right though the commercial and business centre of town,' as one local put it. The event gained great fame and crowds came flocking to enjoy the brief but energetic parade. However, since one of the pubs closed the occasion is temporarily in abeyance, but plans are afoot to challenge the record again in the twenty-first century.

From the early 1900s, a woollen mill gave employment and prosperity to Dripsey, the machinery operated by the fast-flowing river producing fine rugs, blankets and tweeds. Today the mill is silent, small local industry being no match for huge international commercial enterprises, but you can still see the old sheds and machinery down by the river bank, and imagine what a busy place it must have been. A little way upstream are two castles side by side: relatively modern Dripsey, still owned by the O'Shaughnessys who ran the mill, and, next to it, ruined Carrignamuck. The real showpiece castle on this road, though, has to be Carrigadrohid, which stands dramatically on a rocky outcrop in the river beyond Coachford, clearly controlling the arched bridge which crosses the Lee here. There would have been little chance of a medieval farmer passing by with a loaded cart for market without paying dues to the reigning chieftain who presumably kept the door open and a sharp eye up and down the road in both

directions night and day. Coachford too, a literal translation of the Irish, Áth an Chóiste, keeps the memory of a later time when lumbering Victorian passenger coaches changed horses here before crossing the river at a shallow fording point en route for Macroom and Killarney.

Kilcrea to Macroom

The N22 to the south, on the other hand, running along the low-lying Bride valley, where at dawn the rising mist shrouds the landscape in mystery, and at dusk you might be fortunate enough to see a barn owl floating on silent wings, offers temptations too, one of the best being Kilcrea. You can't see it from the main road; you have to turn down a narrow side lane to the left, which may or

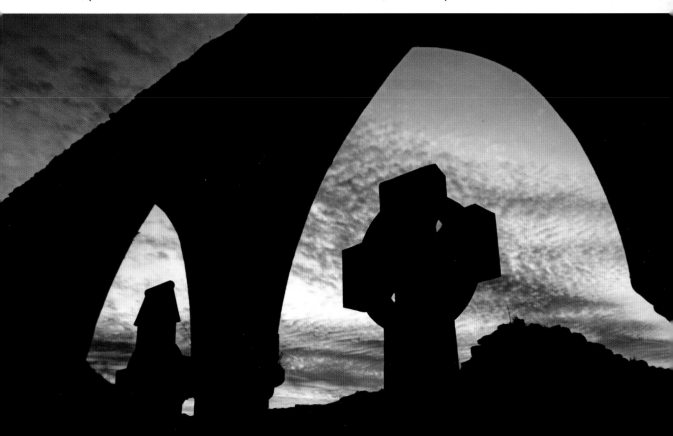

may not be signposted, depending on your luck, and tackle quite a few twists and turns before arriving at a little hump-backed bridge over the river Bride. On one side stands the friary, on the other the castle. Which one first?

Kilcrea (Church of Cré) may originally have been a nunnery before Cormac Láidir McCarthy built the abbey for the Franciscans in 1465. His own castle of Kilcrea was probably built a little earlier. An energetic creator of castellated establishments this Cormac, since Blarney and Carrignamuck are also credited to his zest for building. It didn't do him much good in the end though, as he was murdered at the last-named residence by his brother and nephews. As its founder, his tomb is in the abbey. Art Ó Laoghaire is buried here too – 'Caoineadh Airt uí Laoghaire', the agonised and vengeful lament composed by his wife, Eibhlín Dubh Ní Chonaill, after his death at the hands of an English official, is regarded as one of the greatest love poems in the Irish language.

Kilcrea is a peaceful bywater now, with both friary and castle in comparative ruin, but once it must have hummed with industry and energy, armed men riding to and from the castle keep, cooks preparing food, boys tending flocks, nobles and their ladies taking the air, merchants bringing supplies in heavy carts, monks chanting in the church or delicately illuminating exquisite manuscripts. Every abbey indeed was a little world in itself, and every castle no less so, since the upkeep of either required huge resources in both people and materials. In

summer months, when the fields are golden with ripening crops, you can stand on the bridge and trace the tiny winding pathway, worn by centuries of use, heading through the corn, directly to the castle on its rocky outcrop by the river. No matter what the crop, the path shows through. It's there in winter too, of course, but is etched most vividly against the striking contrast of waving corn. The long valley in which both friary and castle are set was once the Great Bog of Kilcrea, almost impossible for travellers to cross.

Opposite: The grain stalks are ripening, but the centuries-old pathway to Kilcrea Castle cannot be hidden, whatever the season, whatever the crop.
Below: The barn owl can still sometimes be seen at dusk, floating on silent wings along the river fields of the Lee valley, or perching on a ruined building.

Standing alone in a field nearby is ruined Kilcrea House, dating from the late eighteenth century. Now deserted save for wheeling jackdaws, once there would have been a gravelled driveway leading to its front door, and carriages rolling out to meet important guests coming by train from Cork on the old Macroom line. Kilcrea railway station closed in the 1950s, but the station house can still be seen, now on a disused loop off the main road, close to the old post office.

Crookstown, with yet another castle, is where St Finbarr, patron saint of Cork, is supposed to have been born around the fifth century AD, and a side road here leads to Béal na Bláth where Michael Collins, commander in chief of the Irish army and promoter of the Irish Free State, died in an ambush in August 1922. Just before Lissarda is an ingenious example of the ancient and the modern living in perfect harmony: a garden wall fronting the main road has been carefully built

around a standing stone erected long before roads were ever dreamed of. At Dunisky causeway, which crosses the Lee beyond Lissarda, the full extent of a 1950s hydro-electric flooding scheme can be seen encapsulated in the single image of a little bridge standing alone in the midst of the lake. This bridge once crossed the little Buingea river, and when the water is very low, it is possible to walk out and give it the comfort of footsteps and company for a while. Over on the northern bank, where it would once have kept an eye on the busy traffic of a river valley but now stands with its feet almost in the water, is the Elizabethan tower house of Mashanaglass, slowly crumbling into the surrounding bracken and brambles with the passing years.

Whether you take the high road or the low road comes to the same thing eventually, as they meet at the bridge just east of Macroom. Long ago the gathering place for the druids of Munster, Macroom is now a classic Irish market town, with a huge square for the holding of fairs right outside the castle gates and the original market trading house (now the town hall) still standing in its centre. The medieval castle was built by the McCarthys and, with many adaptations and extensions as life became more comfortable, survived right through to the 1920s when it was burned by the anti-Treaty forces shortly after

Above: Ruined Macroom Castle still stands proudly above the bridge over the Sullane, which links the town of Macroom with the once separate community of Masseytown.

Sometimes at evening the
mists rise from the river fields
to swathe around the trees
and reach upwards to the
setting sun with grey ghostly
fingers.

Below: The Gearagh, now a protected reserve, offers shelter and safety for wildlife to rear their families in peace.

the Irish Free State was established. The spacious grounds running down to the river are now maintained by the town as a public park. Admiral Sir William Penn, father of the founder of Pennsylvania, was born in Macroom.

It's worth looking behind the busy main street here to discover little alleys, laneways, surprising connections between one part of the town and another, that you would never suspect existed if you just drove through without stopping. Features like this are characteristic of old towns that developed gradually and organically rather than being planned and laid out on a handy but soulless grid system. There is quite a bit of evidence of the railway days here too for anyone with a sharp eye – the former station yard, now the bus station, a row of buildings called Railway View, an unexpected arch that once carried the line over a laneway on the eastern edge of town. The Cork–Macroom line ran from 1866 to 1953, although for the last twenty years of its service it carried goods only, the loyalty of its former passengers having already been alienated by the convenience of the motor bus and car.

Macroom castle guards the bridge over the Sullane, which here gives itself up to the mightier flood of the Lee. Across the bridge was once an entirely separate community, Masseytown, lorded over by the magnificent Mount Massey, which even had its own special song of praise.

I long to remember those bright days of joy
Which sweetly with joy I beguiled
The friends who frequented my old cabin floor,
And comrades I loved when a child.

How I long for to roam by Mount Massey's green groves
Or poach by the light of the moon
That spot of my birth, there's no equal on earth,
Mount Massey, the pride of Macroom.   *(Traditional ballad)*

Mount Massey is now a ruin, and Masseytown has more or less become part of Macroom, although there is always that pride of separate identity, emphasised by the triple-arched bridge over the Sullane.

A turn to the south west on to the R584 at Hartnett's Cross, just before Macroom, leads to Inchigeelagh, Ballingeary, Gougane Barra, the Pass of Keimaneigh and eventually Bantry. Right on Macroom's doorstep, though, is the strangely compelling Gearagh.

The Gearagh

A flooded forest, a lake, a drowned landscape, a haven for wild birds, a place apart – the Gearagh, or An Gaoire, an old Irish name for a wooded river – is all of

Above: Tree stumps are all that remain of a once great alluvial forest, drowned by a hydro-electric scheme. In former times, moonshiners were said to distil their sought-after product on tiny islands on the Gearagh.

these and more. It is, in fact, the remains of the only ancient post-glacial alluvial forest in Western Europe, formed at the end of the last Ice Age. Up to the 1950s it was a magical region of water and trees, uncountable tiny islands and channels, secretive, mysterious and difficult of access. Legends of the Gearagh were legion, one of the most enduring being that of Seán Rua na Gaoire, a sort of Robin Hood lawbreaker who robbed the rich, helped the poor, and could disappear into the wilderness without trace whenever the forces of authority sought to trap him. Right up to the twentieth century, moonshiners distilled their liquor here, it was said, and tiny rickety bridges made of branches, linking one island with the next, were pointed out as evidence. Moonshine or poteen, an illegal spirit, is inextricably part of Irish tradition (among other things, it was held to be the only known cure for influenza, if taken as a hot toddy), and where better to

Opposite: Midwinter sunrise in a remote corner of the Gearagh. **Below:** After a frosty night, this old green lane near Macroom is tinged with silver.

conduct the slow process of distillation than on a tiny island where unfriendly visitors could be seen approaching from a long way away, and an escape made swiftly?

Despite the disproportionate amount of water and marsh to dry land, a whole community lived in and around the Gearagh for centuries, raising their families, plying their trades, paddling among the complexity of channels in specially-designed flat-bottomed boats. But then came proposals for a hydro-electric scheme and the flooding of the Lee valley. Families that had lived there for generations had perforce to leave and watch, grieving, as the waters slowly rose and drowned their fields, their homes, the paths they knew so well.

It can't be denied that where human beings lost out, nature benefited. Today the Gearagh is a haven for birds, animals and rare plants. Geese and swans come to spend the winter in the mild climate of these rich feeding grounds, while countless other species use it as a stopover to rest and recover before continuing their long journeys south or north, depending on the season. Badgers, otters, foxes and rabbits roam its wild places with no fear. The Gearagh

is now protected as a statutory nature reserve, a Ramsar site (listed under the Convention of Wetlands adopted following an international conference in Ramsar, Iran, 1971), and a biogenetic reserve (an international designation for natural habitats that are especially valuable for nature conservation in Europe). Birdwatchers, plant specialists and nature lovers come here all year round to explore its mysteries, and it is a popular location for walkers and families out for the day.

Only the old track running through its heart, now grassy and shaded with overhanging trees, gives a clue to an earlier time, more domestic uses. Sometimes too, after a particularly dry summer, the network of subsidiary tracks, little field systems, even the original maze of streams which once formed this other-worldly landscape, reveal themselves. For a short while you can walk the old pathways and tracks, can imagine that the Gearagh is once again echoing to the shouts of children, the clucking of hens at a cottage door, the creak of a turf cart, all the sounds of a living, thriving community. At evening, when the setting sun throws the mountains into dramatic relief, and the

Above: The old road through the Gearagh. Once busy with everyday rural life, now a peaceful backwater, do ghosts still walk its familiar route on moonlit nights? **Opposite:** West Cork's only *crannóg* or lake dwelling, on Lough Allua.

black outlines of the ancient tree stumps are etched against the sky, the fluting call of a curlew sounds like a lament for a vanished, simpler world. That's the time you might see the old road opening up before you.

'The old road' is a much-loved tradition in Irish lore. Sometimes it refers to an almost-forgotten former route, now slowly being taken back by the countryside, as at the Gearagh, but it can also refer to other-worldly pathways which appear only at certain times of the year and always at night. When the moon is full, or around the time of the solstice, you might see these roads slowly glimmering back into reality, stretching across a waste of desolate bogland, or up a craggy mountainside. It's said that if you follow, they will lead you to the camp of the Fianna, the legendary warriors of ancient Ireland, to the court of

From right to left, the peaks of Doughill, Douce, and Shehy form a dramatic backdrop at sunset to the Gearagh's waterlands with their evocative tree stumps, the only remnant of an ancient alluvial forest which once covered this landscape.

long-gone High Kings, or even to Tír na nÓg itself, the Land of Youth. Undoubtedly one of the Gearagh 'old roads' must lead to the fairy mountain of Shehy, its peak clearly visible beyond the western end of the Gearagh at sunset, where that demonic black horse, the Pouka, is reputed to make his home. In fairness to the Pouka, he is by no means as bad a character as the Scottish water kelpie, who is wont to drag unwary folk down into bog holes and drown them. Our Pouka will simply throw you on his back and take you galloping to the far side of the mountain if he's of a mind, usually dumping you in a muddy mire before dawn, to make your own way home. One imagines that many a man who had imbibed more freely than wisely at the local hostelry must have used that excuse the following morning to an irate wife.

Inchigeelagh to Ballingeary

Just before Inchigeelagh, in a townland formerly known as Iveleary, the traditional home of the O'Leary clan, an inconspicuous grassy laneway leads down to the riverbank at a former fording point for farm carts and tractors. There is a narrow footbridge to enable you to cross dry shod now (cars, though, have to make a long detour around by country roads), but the real attraction is Carrignacurra, usually called a castle, but more correctly a tower house built by the O'Learys, watching over the river from its strategic high rock. There is a legend here, and a ghost. The last of the O'Leary chieftains rode forth to battle from Carrignacurra in the seventeenth century, but alas never came back. It is said that his wife still waits, and can sometimes be seen at dusk, looking out for her husband's return.

The little stone pier just beyond Inchigeelagh always has a couple of blue-painted wooden boats moored in the rippling water, waiting for hire. Beyond the pier, the river winds onward between undulating green hills, round a rocky corner and out of sight, positively inviting you to seize oars, commandeer a craft and set out to explore by river rather than by road. If you did, then you would soon find the little waterway broadening into Lough Allua which holds

Opposite: Carrignacurra Castle, ancestral home of the O'Leary clan, on a high rock above the fording place on the river Lee. **Below:** Lough Allua is reputed to be the home of a cunning serpent or dragon, banished from Gougane Barra by St Finbarr.

a real rarity for West Cork, a *crannóg*.

Crannógs, or lake dwellings, are relatively numerous in the lake-dotted regions further north in Ireland, but this one, in the delightfully named townland of Tirnaspideoige, or 'Land of the Robins', is the sole example in West Cork. The small trees and scrub that now cover its surface disguise the fact that this is a man-made structure, built on wooden piles driven into the bottom of the lake. They were, in all likelihood, built for protective purposes, with a bridge which could be removed when danger threatened.

It's at Tirnaspideoige that you enter the Muskerry Gaeltacht, one of the regions where our native language is still spoken naturally, and you'll see signs in Irish rather than English on hoardings, shop frontages, notice boards. Muskerry Irish is soft and lilting, and can sound quite different to anyone accustomed to that spoken in the west of Ireland or further north. It's not that there is so much difference in the words used, but more in the inflection, the accent, the

pronunciation. The Muskerry Gaeltacht, named for the ancient barony of Múscraí, is an area roughly bounded by the bustling market towns of Ballyvourney to the north and Ballingeary to the south, with the tiny communities of Coolea, Gougane Barra, Keimaneigh, Kilnamartyra and Renaniree tucked into various points between.

There is a smaller road running along the south side of Lough Allua, twisting wildly as it climbs and drops from little hills to valleys, but getting to Ballingeary all the same, albeit taking a little longer. It's a quiet and rural way to choose, with apple blossom scenting the air in May and rich ripe blackberries for the picking along the old stone walls and hedgerows in August. (Just remember never to pick blackberries after Michaelmas, as that's when the devil throws his cloak over them, spoiling their flavour entirely.)

Whether you take the north or the south road, a splendid clapper bridge may be seen spanning the Lee by Ballingeary, a village which comes alive in summer with thousands of students seeking to improve their Irish language skills. From here onwards, the pull of Gougane Barra is palpable, and indeed the magnificent circle of mountains which shelters it has been visible for some time on the road from Inchigeelagh. Just a few more miles on the main road, and then the signpost points right, taking you on a narrow track into the heart of the hidden valley.

Gougane Barra

Even the greatest cynic would have to admit that Gougane possesses something very special – a sense of apartness, of peace, quiet, restful tranquillity. Undeniably it gets plenty of visitors, especially on weekends, while on Pattern Sunday in

Opposite: Hidden away in a sheltering circle of mountains, Gougane Barra is a legendary spot, miraculously unchanged over the centuries. **Below:** A rainbow spans the lake at Gougane.

late September (celebrating St Finbarr's feast day) you would want to get here early if you hoped to find even a parking place; but go if you can at a quiet time, say midweek in May, and you'll never want to leave. The writer and artist Robert Gibbings had a deep love for Gougane and stayed there many times in the 1940s and 50s, immortalising the local characters and capturing their wonderful dialogue to great effect in books like *Lovely is the Lee* and *Sweet Cork of Thee*.

Gougane, or Inis Irce, to give it its old name, is likely to have been a place of pilgrimage and worship long before Christianity. For one thing, it is the source of the river Lee. Any source of a great river was a powerful site in ancient Ireland, and when you add the encircling mountains – it's actually a cirque, very like that of Gavarnie in the Pyrenees – and the tiny island floating in the dark lake, it's not difficult to see the spell it must have cast on our ancestors. It still casts that spell today, whatever religious beliefs currently hold sway.

(Interestingly, the devil is supposed to have visited Gougane once, according to a local legend recorded by Gibbings. In a farmhouse right in the centre of the valley, as several brothers sat playing cards and drinking late one night, a great black THING, wrapped in chains, bounded down the chimney, leapt through the house and out the door. Sadly, the old farmhouse was later demolished, in order

Opposite: Gougane is the source of the mighty river Lee, which here is no more than a peaceful clear stream flowing between moss and ferns. **Below:** Trees have grown up where fields were once tilled, their roots clasping and preserving the ancient stone walls.

to build modern facilities for visitors at this location in the forest park, but you can keep the incident in mind should you need to make use of it.)

From far back in the mists of time right down to the present day, travellers have come – still come – to Gougane to worship, ask favours, give thanks, seek peace. Today's visitors come by road, whether by the narrow winding route over the hills from Ballyvourney on the Killarney road, from Ballingeary, or up from Bantry through the Pass of Keimaneigh. There is another, older route though, definitely only for the hiker, and a courageous one at that, which brings you over the shoulder of Conigar mountain from Gowlane bridge on the Coomhola Pass in Kerry, and down into the valley by a steep grassy track. In earlier times it was a secret road, a means of getting in or out known only to the few, which led from the Poll, a hidden glen above the top of the valley, up a ravine of huge tumbled rocks known as the Devil's Staircase, and thence across the mountains to Kerry. In times of conflict, many an Irish patriot made his escape from pursuing soldiery this way. You can still see the Staircase if you make the steep climb up through the woods to the Poll, but ascending this rocky challenge isn't desirable or even necessary, since an excellent marked footpath, part of the Beara Way, takes a safer route over the top. This route can be accessed just beside what must be the most delightful of public conveniences ever to be seen anywhere. Round, thatched, and utterly charming, it's a deserving recipient of tourism awards. (And no, it's

quite separate to the one built on the site of the farmhouse said to have been visited by the devil, which is in the depths of the forest park. Just so you know.)

Before the valley was forested in the mid-twentieth century, it was farmed, and there were many tiny fields here, with winding laneways connecting crops and cattle with old-world cottages and farmhouses. Today, as you wander in the green depths of the woods, the dim light slowly reveals the shape of old stone walls, now so covered with moss they seem to have been almost completely absorbed into the natural landscape. Foxgloves and ferns borrow them for support, tree roots clasp them, and hold in place the rocks set there by toil-worn hands a century and more ago. Walking a path, you become aware that you are echoing the footsteps of many a tired labourer wending his way home at evening from a hard day's work. And again and again you meet the little Lee, still only a gurgling baby at this point, dancing its way down the valley. Although various writers have fastened upon one location or another, it is almost impossible, in fact, to be certain where the Lee actually begins. The truth is that uncountable streams converge from the mountainsides, gradually becoming one before the lake is reached.

There is a green island in lone Gougane Barra,
Where Allua of songs rushes forth as an arrow.
In deep-valley'd Desmond, a thousand wild fountains
Come down to that lake from their home in the mountains…
(J J Callanan c. 1825)

Above: This immensely tall standing stone can be found right on the edge of a farmyard, in the hills between Gougane and Ballyvourney.

Legend holds that when St Finbarr first came to Gougane, he found a serpent already in residence there before him, living in the depths of the lake. As is so often the habit of holy hermits though, Finbarr didn't even consider peaceful co-existence but straightaway seized the beast and threw it out of the valley. It flew through the air and landed with such force, between Inchigeelagh and Ballingeary, that a deep hole was created by the impact. Given the rainfall of

West Cork, the hole soon filled up, and became Lough Allua. And is the serpent still there? Nobody has reported seeing him disporting himself around the *crannóg* lately, so he may well have crept silently back to Gougane. It's only a matter of time before someone sees him, perhaps surfacing at dusk to patrol the boundaries of his rightful home.

As befits such a magical place, the valley even had its own wise woman and its own philosopher. Two legendary figures of Gougane Barra in the 1930s and 1940s were the Tailor and Ansty. Immortalised in Eric Cross's book of the same name, this elderly Irish-speaking husband and wife were an irresistible magnet for students, lovers of the old ways, anyone in search of good conversation and lively talk. Their tiny cottage just at the entrance to the great amphitheatre of Gougane, was packed every night and the Tailor was in his element as he held forth on ancient traditions, customs, stories and legends, while Ansty bustled back and forth with sweeping brush and bucket, pausing only to give vent to some caustic rejoinder. '*Glac bog an saol agus glacfaidh an saol bog tú*' (Take the world fine and aisy, and the world will take you the same), was his favourite phrase, while her riposte was usually along the lines of, 'Would you listen to him sitting there talking and not doing a stroke of work!' They were a perfect foil for one another and it is a matter of great sadness to this day that the publication of Cross's book caused such disruption of their peaceful life. Ironically, since it was published in English, and thereby accessible to all, the Irish government of the day immediately decided that its rich colourful language and natural discussion of country matters was shameful, and banned it. (Presumably if it had been in the original Irish, they wouldn't have been so worried.) Clergy then descended on the bewildered old couple and forced them to burn their copy of the book. All that happened, however, a long time ago. The book, now a minor classic, is reprinted, the Tailor's Irish-speaking recollections are preserved for future generations by the Irish Folklore Commission, and the couple sleep peacefully in the tiny graveyard at Gougane. The local hotel stages adaptations of the book each summer in a marquee by the lake, and the text has even been translated into French (Joëlle Gac 2008). Writer Eileen O'Faolain turned one tale she heard from the Tailor into the magical children's story, *The King of the Cats*.

There are those even today who claim to have glimpsed now and again Ansty's upright little figure in its sweeping West Cork cloak making its way up across the stony hillside, followed by her faithful black cat, as she still watches over their beloved patch 'in the townland of Garrynapeaka, in the district of Inchigeelagh, in

Opposite: The Pass of Keimaneigh is a deep, tree-lined pass through the mountains. From here, the road leads down to Bantry and the sea.

Below: Togher Castle, on the flat fields before the road rises to the Cousane Gap, embodies in its name the memory of an ancient wooden trackway across marshland. **Opposite:** An almost-forgotten stone circle near Togher Castle holds its own secrets of the past.

the parish of Iveleary, in the barony of West Muskerry, in the county of Cork, in the province of Munster,' as the Tailor, with an eye to an admiring audience, was wont to style their address.

For the adventurous, a narrow, twisting and distinctly nerve-racking but still driveable road leads up out of the valley to the north (do stop to admire the lovely old clapper bridge leading across a stream to a farmyard at the foot of the climb), connecting eventually, and after many adventures, with the N22 linking Cork and Killarney. Not a route to venture after dark, it travels across high moorland where flocks of sheep scatter at the sight of a car and trees bent double by the wind cling to bare rock. Right at the top, a dramatically tall standing stone can be found, sited rather prosaically on the edge of a working farmyard; the farmer, fortunately, is used to visitors bumping confusedly into his yard and asking for directions.

Gougane, once visited, is very hard to leave. It's a matter of deep thankfulness that, although visitors have been coming here time out of mind, it is still wonderfully unspoiled, unchanged. There are no blatant tourist attractions, no glitz, no overt commercial enterprises. Gougane remains, as it always has been, a genuine place of outstanding natural beauty and peace. You get the distinct feeling, talking to the family who have owned and run the hotel here for generations, or to the couple who take bookings for weddings in the tiny church on the island, or indeed anyone who lives in the valley, that they regard it as a haven to be protected, maintained, kept unspoiled for all those who come seeking peace and refreshment for the soul.

Keimaneigh to Bantry

The sadness of leaving Gougane is, however, compensated for somewhat by the rather splendid Pass of Keimaneigh (from Céim an Fhia, 'the Leap of the Deer') which you enter immediately on quitting the valley and turning right. It's a delight to drive through, all the more so because it is so unexpected and relatively unknown. It may not be the Grand Canyon or the Ronda, but Keimaneigh would certainly give the Cheddar Gorge a good run for its money.

This extraordinary chasm … is about a mile in length, and from the minute correspondence and similarity of the strata on each side, appears to have been rent in the mountain by some convulsion of nature. The rock on both sides rises in a direction nearly perpendicular to the height of 100 feet, and in the fissures the arbutus, holly, yew, ivy, and various evergreens have taken root, and with several rare plants thrive with the greatest luxuriance. The surrounding rocks are of the schistus formation, varying in colour from pale ash to the brightest vermilion …
(Topographical Dictionary of Ireland, by Samuel Lewis, 1837)

Like any pass through the mountains, it's a watershed: entering from the Gougane side, you see a busy little stream rushing down to join the infant Lee as it leaves the lake of its birth, while on the other side, where the landscape opens out dramatically and the road runs steeply down towards Kealkill, the Owvane river tumbles through the rocky hillside on its way to Bantry.

Of course this isn't the only way to go, the only route to choose. Wherever you

Opposite: Kinneigh round tower is unique in having a hexagonal base. It was originally part of a seventh-century monastery, some surrounding walls of which still stand. **Above:** Raindrops, never very far away in West Cork, bring jewelled beauty to wild grasses

drive in this part of the world, there are decisions to be made at every junction, alternative tempting routes to follow. Back near Macroom, a turn to the left at Toon Bridge leads past the site of the 1920 Kilmichael ambush during the War of Independence, towards Dunmanway and Drimoleague. There is an unexpected little remnant of past times in Drimoleague – turn right into a car park in the centre of town and you'll discover the old railway station, lovingly maintained, dozing peacefully, one ear cocked for the whistle of the down train from Cork, its grass-covered platform waiting for passengers who stopped travelling in 1960. (That's the West Cork Railway, not on any account to be confused with the Cork–Macroom Direct Railway – both erstwhile companies would turn in their separate graves if you thought they were the same thing.) Or turn right before Dunmanway and head over the high Cousane Gap towards the coast. En route to the gap, while still in the flat lowlands, you'll pass Togher Castle, its name (meaning as it does an ancient wooden trackway) holding the exciting possibility of future rewarding archaeological finds underneath this marshy landscape. A bit of searching in the side lanes near Togher (it helps to have the OS map in hand) will reveal a fine stone circle. Or go further south and discover Kinneigh Round Tower on the road towards Enniskean. This is the only one known to be built on a hexagonal shape for the lower part and the more usual round form for the rest of its height. It overlooks St Bartholomew's church today, but was originally part of the monastery founded by St Mocholmóg in the year AD 619, according to the Annals of Cork. The original wall which surrounded the monastery grounds still survives.

You get the feeling that JRR Tolkien must surely have had this peaceful region of West Cork very much in mind when he created Middle Earth, and especially the Shire. There are the little tilled fields, the hedges and the winding lanes, here the welcoming inns that old Gaffer Gamgee surely must have frequented. Green woodlands there are aplenty, where elves might well be encountered at dusk, and many a shallow ford across chuckling rivers where a safe crossing might be made by weary hobbits and heavily-laden ponies. Lough Allua, with its *crannóg*, could be the original of Lake Town – complete with threatening serpent. The strange and mysterious Gearagh with its drowned forest must surely have served as the original of the marsh crossed by the Ring Bearers. (Indeed the folklore of the Gearagh includes the description of a condition known as the *meascán maraíocht* which made unwary travellers confused and unable to tell which way to go.) Certainly tree-filled Gougane could be the magical Rivendell, and its welcoming hotel is the Last Homely House, no doubt about that.

'Not all those who wander are lost,' as the aforementioned Tolkien observed, and that is delightfully the case in this part of West Cork. There is one thing certain though. Wherever you choose to wander, whether you take the road through Inchigeelagh, cross the Cousane Gap, or wander through Dunmanway and Drimoleague, it comes to the same thing in the end. They all meet up, sooner or later, at Bantry Bay. But that's an exploration for another day.

CHAPTER II

THE ROAD WINDS WEST

OLD HEAD, BALTIMORE, THE ISLANDS

A coastline that twists as freely as a soaring gull, a patchwork of small fields with the salt spray on their faces. A safe harbour for every day in the year, a castle for every Sunday. And more islands than a lifetime could explore.

Pages 44-45: Looking back over the Seven Heads towards the Old Head of Kinsale.
Below: The Old Head of Kinsale, dramatically etched against a dark backdrop and a silver sea.

J ust as the Lee makes a natural northern border for West Cork, so too does the Bandon river mark the dividing line on the east. Curving down from the busy market town of Bandon, past Downdaniel castle, it turns south at picture-book Innishannon and heads for the ocean. The river divides the Old Head of Kinsale from the popular tourist town of Kinsale itself, which is the location of much sailing activity, but once you cross the bridge over the river you are heading for the wilds of West Cork.

Well known writer Alice Taylor, author of the much-loved *To School through the Fields* as well as many other works, is in no doubt whatsoever as to where exactly West Cork begins – in her home town of Innishannon. 'Way back, you see, this was the first fordable crossing point of the river Bandon and the village here simply grew up around the ford, in the most natural of ways,' she told me. Lord Shannon, she said, certainly planned and built a model village for the linen industry here in the eighteenth century (and an open space by the river is still called the Bleaching Green), but the river crossing had already laid the thriving foundations. 'Everyone heading up to Cork with pack ponies or

maybe with heavy loads on their own backs, this was the place they would cross. And in the same way, anyone going west would head for here to cross the Bandon river. Once over, you were in West Cork.' Let other towns object as they may: Innishannon, claims Alice Taylor, can with confidence call itself the Gateway to West Cork.

From here the river broadens out and moves slowly and peacefully down past the castle of Ship Pool (said to be haunted), by Long Quay, Black Quay, Kilmacsimon on the opposite bank, all, like Ship Pool, demonstrating a long link with boats and trading. And doubtless many more forgotten little piers, landing places, where for centuries small boats tied up, lie hidden along the banks. The river brought commerce and prosperity to the Bandon region but it also took much away: the Earl of Cork and other English settlers were active in the felling of trees and floating the timber downriver to the sea and across to Britain where demand was constant. Even today, when much replanting has taken place, it's a far cry from the time when all of Ireland was heavily forested.

Old Head of Kinsale

Looking at the spectacular Old Head of Kinsale, or Downmacpatrick, jutting arrogantly out into the Atlantic, it's easy to believe it was once the mighty seat of royalty. There are historical references connecting it with the Eireann Celtic tribe who may have been the first to light their beacons on the clifftops here. There are still traces of hut settlements dating from as far back as the later Iron Age, as well as those of the medieval monks who continued the tradition of keeping beacons burning. The remaining traces of fortifying walls and an old castle at the narrowest part of the promontory, where the beacons would originally have been placed, date from the thirteenth century and the Anglo-Norman de Courceys. The lighthouse has been automatic since 1987, yet some visitors claim to have

Below: It is said that the old lighthouse keepers still maintain a ghostly presence at the Old Head lighthouse, heard but never seen. Here all looks innocent enough amid drifts of summer flowers.

heard invisible seaboots clumping up and down the old steps. Perhaps the old lighthouse keepers still take their responsibilities seriously, and don't trust modern technology to perform adequately the job they once carried out by night and day, fair weather and foul.

The old signal tower standing near the ruined castle is a reminder of the importance throughout the ages of this headland in discovering enemies approaching by sea, be it Spanish galleons or Napoleonic battleships. In an age long before the advent of swift electronic communications, a clear day and keen eyesight was often all the warning you could expect. One imagines that in times of threat, swift horses were kept in readiness to carry the news to forces further inland that danger was on the way.

Beacons or no, foggy weather and the meeting of two tidal races can make this a risky place to sail past, and there are all too many records of shipwrecks. When, in 1892, the *City of Chicago* went aground on the rocks, passengers, including many ladies in voluminous dresses, were saved by valiantly climbing swaying rope ladders thrown down by rescuers from the clifftop far above. The Old Head is also remembered, more tragically, for being the nearest land point to the

sinking of the *Lusitania* in 1915, the act which was responsible for bringing the United States into the First World War. It is said that people were actually able to watch from the headland, horrified and unable to do anything to help, as the ship went down on a sunny afternoon within sight of shore.

You wouldn't suspect it, but there are several natural tunnels running right underneath the Old Head. These are just about navigable on a low tide, in a shallow-draught boat or canoe, and it is an eerie experience to land on a tiny gravel beach in the deep heart of the headland, with only the faintest star of light behind or in front to show the way out. Basking sharks often use these subterranean passages, their rough sandpaper-like skin capable of inflicting serious damage on a rubber dinghy. It is really inadvisable to go looking for these tunnels though, unless you are with an experienced local boatman. Being caught inside on a rising tide doesn't bear thinking about. The clue to the existence of the tunnels lies in the local place names which, as so often, quietly, unobtrusively, record past events, old sites, or former unguessed-at uses for an apparently innocuous landscape. In this case you can see Holeopen Bay East and West marked clearly on the OS map,

Just off the eastern side of the Head lies Bream Rock, and landward of this, although invisible from above, is a tiny sheltered bay and precipitous steps cut in the rock up to a natural spring, used by fishermen out from home for weeks at a time.

The road west follows the magnificent length of Garrettstown beach, a longtime favourite with holidaymakers and surfers, and then around to Kilbrittain, which boasts the oldest inhabited castle in Ireland. The original fortress here on the deep inlet may have been built by the O'Mahonys in the eleventh century, but by the thirteenth it was in the hands of the Norman de Courceys, who rebuilt the basic defensive structure into something more in keeping with their idea of ruling grandeur. The seat of the McCarthy Reaghs from the early fifteenth century, Kilbrittain Castle has been restored, rebuilt and extended by various owners over the centuries. Amy Cahill-O'Brien, the present chatelaine, is proud of having installed underfloor heating, thereby dealing once and for all with that perennial problem for Irish castle dwellers, the damp.

Further south along the eastern shores of the inlet, Coolmain Castle was originally built by the de Courceys in the early 1400s. In the twentieth century, little more than a ruin, it was bought by the American novelist Don Byrne, whose wife came from this area, and then the Hollywood photographer Bob Willoughby, who carried out considerable restoration work. Its most recent owner was Roy Disney, nephew of the legendary Walt.

There are two holy wells close to Flaxford Strand on the coast road round to Timoleague: one by Burren Bridge, the other further up a little side road from the same bridge. These holy wells, often hung with offerings, rags, beads, medals, are a relic of far older beliefs than Christianity, although it isn't likely that many who come to them seeking answers to their prayers are aware of continuing an age-old tradition of worshipping nature spirits.

Timoleague

The ruined abbey effortlessly dominates this long sea inlet, appearing almost to float on the water's edge. At night, with its sharply defined outlines rising into a starry sky, and silence all around save for the call of a lonely curlew, it is incomparable. Founded in the fourteenth century by the Franciscans, the name comes from the Irish, Tigh Molaga, or 'The House of Molaga', the man credited

with bringing beekeeping and honey production to Ireland. If indeed he did, he must have succeeded at exceptional speed, since honey is mentioned in the earliest surviving texts as an everyday staple, a sweetener long before sugar was known here, and the essential ingredient for that most popular drink, mead. Honey and beekeeping are still very much part of Irish country life: in fact a small journal entitled *An Beacaire* (The Beekeeper), established in 1881, is still in publication, and you may find its unassuming green cover competing quietly with modern glossy magazines in country newsagents.

In its day, Timoleague was one of the largest and most important of the religious houses in Ireland. Suppressed, like all the others, during the Reformation, it proved its staying power. Its monks remained discreetly and quietly in the region, and then returned in 1604 to repair the damage and bring the old house back to life. The fabulous Book of Lismore was in the keeping of Timoleague Abbey in 1629. This legendary artefact was only rediscovered in 1814, hidden behind a wall at Lismore Castle, local *pied-à-terre* of the Dukes of Devonshire, doubtless placed there for safekeeping during some perceived period of danger. It is now held at the Duke of Devonshire's seat, Chatsworth, in England. Its original name, though, was *Leabhar Mhic Cárthaigh Riabhaigh* or

'The Book of the McCarthy Reaghs'. (The wedge of land reaching from Enniskean down to Ring was strong McCarthy territory, effectively and strategically dividing two of the settler Barry clans, those at Barryroe and those at Rathbarry.) The great value of the Book of Lismore is that it was compiled from earlier, now lost, texts such as the Book of Monasterboice, as well as other manuscripts. One of the most fascinating of the latter is Leabhar Ser Marco Polo, an Irish translation of the intrepid Italian traveller's voyages. It's a salutary reminder, in these days of bulk printing, that in earlier times if a copy were required, every single word of every single document had to be written out by an educated hand. (You also can't help wondering what it must have been like for an Irish monk, hunched over his writing desk in a chilly cell, translating into

his native tongue the colour and fabled riches of the East as described by Marco Polo.) Perhaps coincidentally, Tim Severin, the renowned writer/explorer who famously 'proved by doing' that St Brendan could indeed have sailed to the New World in a leather boat, has made his home here by the sea. An Irish Marco Polo indeed (although Tim hasn't had the benefit of inexhaustible Venetian ducats to speed his explorations).

The village of Timoleague grew up around the abbey throughout the centuries, as such settlements were wont to do, since monks require not only food and drink with cooks to prepare it, but also parchment and vellum, inks, building works, horses, hay, in fact everything a large establishment generally needs. Given its tactical location at the head of a quiet inlet, it is hardly surprising that the monks are rumoured to have done an excellent trade in smuggled Spanish wine too.

Oddly enough, only a few miles along the shore road towards the popular holiday resort of Courtmacsherry, you find the ruins of Abbeymahon, a thirteenth-century Cistercian house. It is unusual to find two religious communities within such a short distance of each other, but Abbeymahon was never as prosperous as Timoleague, and by the fifteenth century was more or less in disuse, only the church continuing to be used for local worship. Today it sits dozing in the sunshine by the water, overgrown with ivy and brambles, but with the outline of fine archways and doorways, and most of the tower still visible, as well as gravestones (including that of Diarmait Mac Cárthaig, son of Domnall Cairbrech, buried here in 1278).

Seven Heads

The Seven Heads peninsula is an extensive and deeply indented area of rugged coastline which stretches from Timoleague through Courtmacsherry, around to Dunworley Bay and on to Barryscove, Ardgehane and Ballinglanna. There is a walking route right around the peninsula, although you'd need a couple of days to do the entire 42.5km. Nothing stopping you doing bits of it as and when you feel like it, though. How and where you count the seven headlands is up to you – there are more than enough to make up the number and still have spares.

The old, almost lost village of Melmane at the northern end of Broad Strand, was once connected to Coolbaun at the southern end by road, but coastal erosion swept the thoroughfare away. You can track it along the beach, and

Opposite: The ruins of thirteenth-century Abbeymahon, a Cistercian monastery, drowse in the sunshine.

rejoin the former highway at Coolbaun, which once bustled with the life of a busy slate quarry but is now quiet and empty. A lifeboat was launched from here on that fateful May day in 1915 to go to the aid of the *Lusitania*. You can still see the old lifeboat station, although this selfless and vital service is now provided from Courtmacsherry. Blind Strand lies beyond, and Lislee, a Barry castle, once stood here, although today no trace remains.

By car, exploring the Seven Heads is an entertaining if time-consuming process of driving down to the sea or the cliff edge on one tiny boreen, then retracing your steps to take the next one, and so on. Very peaceful and full of delightful discoveries, if you don't mind eleven-point turns every so often. On foot, you can take a track across the Coolim cliffs to the next headland, Carrigrour, and from there to the wide sweep of Seven Heads Bay. Birds (and those miraculously possessed of seven-league boots), can hop and skip from one melodiously-named headland to another: Poulna Point to Vregira and Illaunbaun, Reenreagh to Leganagh with its signal tower, and finally round by Phreeson Point to the promontory fort at the head of Dunworley Bay.

Dunworley

The treacherous rocks around this lovely bay have caused many shipwrecks in their time, and generations of children have searched after a storm for the coveted blue beads yielded grudgingly from the depths by one of these casualties. Out of the many possibilities, the two most likely candidates for the beads are the *Rover*, an Algerian pirate ship, thought to have been involved in the Sack of Baltimore before falling foul of the treacherous rocks along this coastline in 1631, and the *Amity*, an African slave trader which was carrying cannon, timber, glass and elephants' tusks when it went down in 1700.

The coast road here takes you round by Ring, once the thriving port for the town of Clonakilty, with Inchydoney Island across the water on your left as you approach Clonakilty. Inchydoney, linked to the mainland by a causeway, is another huge favourite with holidaymakers, its spreading sand dunes and gently-sloping golden sands the very stuff of which childhood memories are made. A rock at the tip of the island is known as Our Lady's Point, and there has long been a tradition here to search for Our Lady's Shells, in reality the skeletons of sea urchins, but (with the eye of faith) displaying an image of the Blessed Virgin on their surface.

The setting sun makes
Inchydoney beach a sea of gold
for horse and rider.

Clonakilty

It's a cheerful and bustling little town is Clon, even though traffic can get a bit jam-packed in its narrow main street at busy times. It's the fate of many small villages that grew and developed at a time when bulk motorised traffic could not have been dreamed of. A one-way system helps a little, and that famed West Cork laid-back approach prevents it ever becoming too serious. You can see the site of Deasy's Quay at the roundabout on the Cork side of town. The Deasy family were brewers and sea-merchants as well as, some said, smugglers. To be fair, it would be hard not to be a smuggler when you lived so conveniently on a quiet coastline and taxes were so high on desirable products such as brandy and fine cloth. Indeed, this bit of Clon is still known as 'little Dunkirk' by older residents, due to the frequent trips made to that French port. The Deasys had a shipyard here too in the nineteenth century.

The Earl of Shannon held Clonakilty from the English Crown in the eighteenth and nineteenth centuries, and seems to have been a fairly benevolent landlord, introducing many improvements. The large water pump known affectionately as the Wheel of Fortune, and which is reputed never to run dry, was his doing, as was the creation of a flourishing linen industry which at its peak employed more than ten thousand. The Friday market was attended by buyers from Cork and Bandon who bought the cloth for English and Scottish clients. The old Linen Hall building still stands, next to the Wheel of Fortune.

Wherever you are going in Clonakilty, sooner or later you're going to find yourself crossing one of its many bridges over the little river

Above: The church of Mary Immaculate stands on the banks of the little river Feale that runs through the town of Clonakilty.

Feale, which bubbles and sparkles right through the town centre. There is something very pleasant about a river running right through the centre of a town, one that has not been covered over or hidden from view by unstoppable progress over the centuries. Elsewhere names like Sand Quay or Quay House are the only visual reminders that the waters of the Atlantic lapped at the very doors of merchants' houses here before road traffic became more important than boats. Boats, in fact, tied up next to Quay House right into the 1970s when this area was filled in to make the ring road. In 1810, The Rev. Horatio Townshend wrote:

There are four large quays at Cloghnikilty, each of which has several lighters constantly at work during the summer months. The proximity of the ocean, though not attended with all the circumstances that favour other maritime situations is, however, of prime and permanent importance. The tide flows up to its quays navigable for small sloops and lighters and though the great accumulation of sand at its mouth renders ingress and egress often difficult and sometimes dangerous, the harbour is, at high water, accessible to brigs and sloops and when attained, a station of perfect security.
(Statistical Survey of the County of Cork)

Above: The region around Clonakilty is a Mecca for birdwatchers and sights like this cloud of wheeling golden plover are often to be seen, as well as rarer birds on passage.

The Clonakilty School of Industry for Girls, teaching the old, traditional handwork skills, used to stand in peaceful Emmet Square. A splendid christening robe made here in 1841 for Queen Victoria's firstborn is now displayed in the National Museum of Ireland. Michael Collins stayed at No. 7, the home of his sister Margaret (whose husband, Patrick O'Driscoll, was editor of the *West Cork People*), when he was attending school in the town.

Clonakilty has always been regarded as a stronghold of that wonderful and highly practical garment, the West Cork cloak, although it was worn throughout the region, and most towns in the late nineteenth and early twentieth century would have boasted at least one cloak-maker. Designed to cover the wearer completely, and thus extravagant in the yardage required, it was usually made of fine black wool twill, lined with black satin (although there are records from earlier times of blue and red cloaks, which must have added a bright touch of colour to the streetscape). The gathered hood could be loosened and worn over the shoulders as a cape, but most women wore it pulled well forward over the face. The traditional cloak was an expensive investment, made to last, and was often passed down from mother to daughter to granddaughter. In the Model Village on the outskirts of Clon, the waxwork model of an old woman wearing just such a cloak sits in a timeless West Cork Railway waiting room, her travelling bags piled at her feet, dozing as she waits for the bell that will tell her the train is on the way. It's a brief moment in the past caught and held preserved for future generations to pause and muse over how much the railway once meant to this region. From the moment Clonakilty station opened in 1886, it became an integral part of local life, providing a vital link for both goods and people, right up to its much-lamented closure on Good Friday 1961. 'On the day of a big match in Cork every man in town would be up at the station bright and early,' recollected one pub owner, 'and on Fair Day, the crowds would be pouring in on every train. Ah we miss it badly.' The station, now a private house, still stands at the top of a steep hill above the town. Bet it still holds the memories though.

Just north of Clonakilty is the village of Shannonvale, which along with Innishannon owes its name and indeed its existence to Lord Shannon, of the Earl of Cork's family, who laid out both towns and founded a linen industry in each. Today industry is pretty well gone from Shannonvale (although you might want to check the local church for the Harry Clarke stained glass window, the very last to be created by this brilliant artist), but far earlier signs of settlement still stand. Templebryan stone circle is all too easily missed, since it's on the other side of a high bank as you drive out of the village, and somebody (preferably not the driver) has to keep a sharp eye out for the tall grey stones just peeping over the vegetation. It's an interesting circle this, with the stones not tapering as is usual but sharply cut off to leave a flat top. Whether this was the original design, contrary to the norm, or the stones were forcibly altered in a later period, perhaps by some over-zealous clergyman, isn't known. The circle now stands quite happily on the edge of a tilled field, sometimes surrounded by tall maize stalks, sometimes by swaying oats or wheat. Very close by to the north, up a muddy lane past a farmhouse on top of a little hill, is an old circular monastic site with a spectacular

Below: A young Irish draught colt checks that the ancient ogham finger stone and hollowed bullaun stone at Shannonvale have not moved from their grassy enclosure since his last visit.

ogham stone finger pointing to the sky. Close by a bullaun or hollowed stone stands waiting for the age-old rituals to be commenced once more. The fusion of Christian community, standing stone and bullaun is yet another example of how a later religion takes over earlier powerful symbols for its own purposes.

South from Clon, along a causeway renowned among birdwatchers for the vast number of waders to be seen, from the heron standing silent in a pool to clouds of golden plover wheeling in the sky, brings you to Ardfield, where an ancient graveyard holds a stone erected in memory of the parents of a colourful son of the region, Rocky Mountain O'Brien. O'Brien was born and bred at Ardfield, but after taking part in uprisings against the unpopular landlords, had to flee to the New World in the 1860s. Gaining his nickname in mining camps, Rocky settled eventually in the West and became prominent in the North American patriotic movement, fighting tirelessly from across the Atlantic for Ireland's freedom. When he visited Clonakilty once more, in 1901, he was given a hero's welcome, but shadowed closely by British agents fearful of the encouragement he might give to local groups.

Galley Head and Castlefreke

Galley Head or Dundeady stands dramatically high above the sea, overlooking St George's Channel and the two magnificent beaches of Red Strand and Long Strand. Almost an island in itself, it was of high strategic importance in the past, and even today the headland is still defiantly separated from the mainland by the sturdy Norman walls of Dundeady, a castle of the O'Cowhigs. The lighthouse was built in 1875 and, together with the Fastnet, has the distinction of being one of the most powerful in Europe. The illumination it throws landward is unusually wide too, and this, tradition holds, is because the Sultan of Turkey requested that he should be able to enjoy its beams whenever he visited his friends at Castlefreke (see below). It's a nice idea, but more likely that the light was designed to illuminate as far as possible into the wide bays of Clonakilty and Rosscarbery to north and south.

Carmel Browne comes from a long line of lighthouse keepers and actually grew up at Galley Head lighthouse in the 1960s. 'It was a wonderful place to live. There were fifteen of us in the family and we knew every inch of that headland, the best places to play, to sunbathe, to go swimming. A big excitement was when Irish Lights would bring supplies to the old slipway and unload them –

Opposite: Galley Head lighthouse in its magnificent clifftop setting. The black cat and the stonechat in the foreground are clearly guardians of the region.

we'd always go down to help.' Every single one of the children, she says, was keenly aware of the importance of that light, and that it must be kept burning at all times during the dark hours. 'My father, and the other men who were employed there before it went automatic, would work four-hour shifts because that was how often the machinery needed to be wound up for the light to revolve. Many's the night I'd lie snug in bed listening to the wind and rain and thinking of ships travelling safely past Galley Head, watching for our flashing light.' Today two keeper's houses have been adapted for visitors who want to experience the wild beauty of this headland by night as well as day.

Just beyond Galley Head lies Long Strand, and, set back in the fine woodlands behind, the beautifully kept village of Rathbarry and the splendid ruins of Castlefreke. This region gives a marvellous example of how the twists and turns of history are written in the landscape for those who know how to read them. First comes Rathbarry Castle, built in the fifteenth century by the Barry family. This and its lands passed to the Frekes, later Lords of Carbery, in the early 1600s with one of those swift changes of fortune which so characterise lordly life at that time. Attacked by local clans in 1642, in what was to become famed as the longest siege in Irish history, it survived only to be destroyed by Cromwellian forces in 1648. Undeterred, the then Lord Carbery, Sir John Evans Freke, built a new castle on a new site, some little distance away. Hence you find both Rathbarry and Castlefreke rather closer to one another than aristocratic personal space would usually permit. (The same layout obtains beyond Castletownbere, where the original Dunboy Castle stands ruined in the grounds of later Dunboy House.)

Castlefreke was given a Gothic makeover, complete with battlements, by renowned architect Sir Richard Morrison in 1820 and then had almost a century of relative peace, during which a Sprigging School for the making of lace was set up by the then Lady Carbery in the village of Rathbarry. The little low white building still stands, and deservedly won a recent award for its sensitive restoration. It's not likely, alas, that anyone in the area still retains even a folk memory of the old lacemaking skills, passed down from mother to daughter through the generations, but it may be that there are still little boxes of needles, threads, patterns, tucked away in someone's attic, unrecognised for the part they played in easing local poverty in harsher times.

Mary, wife of the 9th Baron Carbery, was a prolific writer, author of, inter alia, *The Children of the Dawn* and *The Farm by Lough Gur*. She was also an enthusiastic

traveller, in her youth crossing Europe in an ox-drawn caravan christened 'Creeping Jenny'.

In 1910 Castlefreke was almost totally destroyed by fire, but determinedly the family had it extensively refurbished in time for the traditional coming-of-age party for John, tenth Lord Carbery. This dashing eccentric, who had clearly inherited his mother's zest for life, learned to fly almost as soon as flying became possible, and gave exhibitions of aerobatics before the outbreak of World War I, whereupon he immediately joined the Royal Flying Corps and served as a pilot throughout the hostilities. There is a well-loved, if apocryphal, local tradition that whenever he landed his plane at Cork he would telephone the local constabulary along his route home and order them to clear the road so that he could bowl along in his open motor car undisturbed and undelayed by donkey carts or herds of cows. Sadly, the difficult postwar years forced him to sell Castlefreke in the 1920s. Since then it has lain in picturesque ruins, a vision which could easily double for Act III of *The Sleeping Beauty* when glimpsed from a distance. Lately, however, restoration work has begun and Castlefreke may well enter yet another stage of its life, again welcoming guests, but this time as a luxury hotel.

The castle is private, but the magnificent Castlefreke woodlands passed into

Below: The cup-marked Burgatia stone stands in a field above the ancient settlement of Rosscarbery.

state ownership after World War II and are now a wonderful place to wander, especially in late spring and early summer when lakes and drifts of bluebells transform this into a fairy realm, or in autumn when the venerable trees, planted by earlier generations of Carberys, take on their russet hues. The Lord Carbery memorial cross, which you will find atop Croghna Hill here, is the largest of its kind in Ireland.

Rosscarbery

The ancient Stone of Burgatia, with its enigmatic cup marks, stands sentinel in the field by the side of the road looking down on the spreading inlet of Rosscarbery. Small though the town is today, only coming alive during the horse fair in late August, it is actually a very old settlement indeed, with Neolithic, Iron and Bronze Age occupants giving way to Early Christian monks. St Fachtna established a monastery here in the sixth century, around which the town grew up. The school attached to the monastery became a famed place of learning, attracting students from all over Europe. A fascinating old Irish poem has survived in The Book of Leinster; 136 lines long, it was written by Airbertach Mac Croisse da Bhrian, a professor at that school, sometime before the year AD 970, the year in which Ross was destroyed by the Danes. In it a surprisingly accurate geographical knowledge of the ancient world is laid out, for example India:

I

*From that great land to the River
Indus westward (is)*

India great and proud:

From the north, from the Hindoo Coosh,

to the strait of Mare Rubrum

II

Known is its excellence on every side.

Its madnets and its diamonds,

Its pearls, its gold dust and its carbuncles

III

Its unicorns of fierce habits

Its soft and balmy breezes;

Its elephants of mightly strength

Its two harvests in one year.

(Source of translation unknown)

Below: Ruined Coppinger's Court, half-hidden by protective trees and shrubs, seems like a scene from a fairytale.

If this is a typical example of the learning being passed on to pupils at Ross, it certainly gives cause for serious reconsideration of those centuries so blithely written off as the Dark Ages. We can only hope that other such priceless fragments may yet be rediscovered, to help us adjust somewhat our smug assumptions about olden times.

Just west of Rosscarbery on the main N71 is a signpost to unique Castle Salem, which happily can be visited since it is now run as a guesthouse. From the avenue, the lovely old manor house, probably built around the same time as Coppinger's Court (see below), stands graciously welcoming; but it conceals behind its charming façade an even earlier history. On the first floor landing, a massive oak door opens right into the Middle Ages – to be more precise, on to the stone flags of a passage high up in the massively thick walls of Benduff Castle, built in 1470, and still retaining its huge fireplace and original arched windows.

Don't believe everything you hear about the discomforts of the Middle Ages, though. Follow a narrow passage set within the thickness of the castle walls and you'll discover not just one but two handy conveniences, set into a corner over a dizzying drop. Lady of the house Margaret Daly always ensures that a supply of sphagnum moss is always kept to hand here, just as it would have been in any well organised medieval castle. Hardly surprising that Castle Salem gets overnight guests from all over the world, eager to see this unique juxtaposition of different eras.

Glandore to Lough Hyne and Skibbereen

If you take the R597 out of Rosscarbery instead, marked for Glandore, keep your eyes open for the striking ivy-clad ruin of Coppinger's Court, set in a valley to the left, below the road, not far from Ross. The Coppingers were an old Viking family who clearly found this pleasant countryside preferable to sailing wild seas and engaging in pitched battles on a nightly basis, and settled down in the fertile valley of Ballyvirine. The impressive and strongly fortified house (said to have had a window for every day of the year, a chimney for every week, and a door for every month) was built sometime after 1612 by Sir Walter Coppinger, determined to bring order and prosperity to the region. Local people weren't as properly grateful as they should have been, however, and his plans received an abrupt check in the 1641 rebellion when the house was attacked and partially burned. Today only the jackdaws raise the echoes around this evocative ruin,

Opposite: Rabbit Island, near
Union Hall. The last family left
the island in the 1970s.

and cows graze the former grounds of Coppinger's Court.

Drombeg stone circle is a little further along the same road, but to be frank it's not the best experience of these mysterious ancient monuments that you could find. It's been tidied up, made too neat, complete with designated car parking and a marked pathway to the site. There are far more untouched and dramatic examples of stone circles to be found on windswept hilltops, half-hidden in woodlands, on mountainsides, throughout West Cork, and you can have them all to yourself. This isn't to say, of course, that Drombeg isn't genuine – it is – but somehow the over-tidying has taken away most if not all of the atmosphere.

Glandore and Union Hall lie only a few miles apart, on opposite sides of Glandore Bay, but couldn't be more different. One is a yachting haven, the other a working fishing port; one is picture-postcard, the other strictly utilitarian. And yet they both share the same waters, make their living from the same sea, whether through tourism or fishing, and each depends on and benefits from the proximity of the other, as members of a close family tend to do.

Picturesque Glandore, with its colourful boats, neat cottages, and lush surrounding greenery probably deserves its reputation as one of Ireland's prettiest villages, and in summer its moorings are crowded with yachts and pleasure boats. The advice always given to sailors navigating into Glandore is to 'avoid Adam and hug Eve', the two rocky islands guarding the entrance to the harbour, since it is only thus you can be sure of making a safe passage through. It's been a settlement for many centuries, doubtless due to the excellent sheltered harbour which offered opportunities to both traders and sailors. The Normans built two castles here in 1215, probably with an eye to more threatening marauders. The local fair was held on a beach close to the village right up to the nineteenth century, the beach being known as Trá an Aonaigh (the Beach of the Fair) in consequence. Many well-to-do and well-known people have summer homes in Glandore, and others flock to enjoy the almost Mediterranean atmosphere of boating and fun.

When you move on to Union Hall, although it is exactly the same bay, the ambience switches instantly from playtime to work. Union Hall is a practical, cheerful little settlement, with a strong community spirit bred of centuries of dealing with the sea in all its moods. There is a large fishing fleet based in the port, and when the trawlers arrive back from a run, huge lorries vie for space on the quayside, loading the fresh catch straight into refrigerated containers to be transported the entire length of the country, and abroad too. It's a good place to hire a small boat for yourself and try your luck with rod and line, while getting an alternative view of the beautiful coastline, or simply fish from the rocks as generations of coastal dwellers have done. Even during the worst of the Famine, those who knew something of the bounty of the sea fared at least a little better than those further inland.

This is the stretch of coastline reputedly haunted by Cliona's Wave, which gives a lonely keening sound as it crashes in foam against the cliffs and rocks. Cliona was a goddess who left the Land of Youth to be with her mortal lover. The gods, however, were not pleased, and as she lay sleeping on the shore, they caused a wave to sweep her out to sea and carry her, against her will, back to her rightful sphere. If you hear the wave sighing here, it's a reminder that Cliona is still longing to return to her lost love.

Castletownshend beckons, but it would be a shame to move on westward without discovering the utter charm of the hidden headlands and bays south of Union Hall. Wander down narrow lanes to Carrigillihy and Squince Harbour, where you can look across to Rabbit Island. The ruined houses here were

occupied by the last of the old island families right up into the 1970s, with three elderly brothers still making their living from fishing. There used to be a holy well here too, and the island's tiny beach is still known as Trá an Tobair, or Well Strand. At Myross there is an old graveyard and from here you can look out to more distant High and Low Island. Low Island, so legend says, was used as a burial ground during times of pestilence, and later during the Famine. Discover Blind Harbour, Reen Point, with its promontory fort, Skiddy Island offshore, and haunted Lough Cluhir. According to The Annals of the Four Masters, a celebrated necromancer, Ivor, the son of Crom, resides within Lough Cluhir, and once every seven years his ship is seen floating on its waters, sails set and pennants flying. It may or may not be good luck to spot Ivor and his ship, but whales and sharks are certainly often spotted cruising past Rabbit Island, and it's pleasant to sit awhile on the cliffs on a sunny day and watch out for them. This area is largely undiscovered (it must be admitted that the lanes are fairly narrow and twisting, more often than not with grass growing in the centre), which makes it wonderfully peaceful.

Above: The steeply sloping main street of Castletownshend has an air of yesteryear.

The road curving up back along the eastern side of Castle Haven and the Narrows, passes Cat Island Quay facing Castletownshend across the water. It is so close you could almost throw a stone to the pebbly shore on the other side, yet a long way round by road. You'd have a small boat if you lived here.

The elegant faded grandeur of Castletownshend is a totally different environment. It's been an enclave of the landed gentry for centuries. The village grew up around the castle built in the seventeenth century by the Townshend family who still own that imposing pile today. You can stay here, and enjoy a sense of the old Irish Big House for yourself if you're so minded.

Castletownshend is, most famously, where Edith Somerville and her cousin Violet Martin lived and wrote, creating together over almost thirty years the unforgettable characters immortalised in the Irish RM hunting stories as well as a number of full-length novels, most notably *The Real Charlotte*. Edith was Master of the West Carbery hunt, a position she thoroughly enjoyed, and which doubtless provided many of the anecdotes for those delightfully colourful stories. Violet Martin died in 1915, but Edith lived on to 1949, continuing to write under their joint names. They are both buried in the graveyard of St Barrahane's church, under simple headstones.

Castletownshend has changed little, outwardly at least, since the time of Somerville and Ross (if you discount, that is, the expensive four-wheel-drives navigating its narrow and steep main street). Those coming to the village for the first time are often taken aback by the considerable challenge presented halfway down this main thoroughfare by two mature sycamore trees right in the middle, comfortably protected by a chest-high stone surround. Other towns might decide to remove awkward barriers. Castletownshend does not. Its forefathers circumnavigated the obstacle, so can today's residents. The solid old stone houses speak of privilege and assurance, as indeed do the three large stone tablets in the church, telling the history of the town's founding families.

Below: Rich yellow lichens decorate the stonework around this once-vital water pump in Castletownshend.

A few miles from Castletownshend on the R596 lies one of the most spectacular prehistoric alignments in West Cork. The stone row at Garranes is magnificent, easily visible from a distance by virtue of its sheer height, atop a hill. Making the effort to scramble across a couple of muddy fields and up the grassy slopes to visit the three tall finger stones in person is immensely worth it. Lofty and silent sentinels, they gaze out across the landscape, impervious to the wind which plays constantly around them. They were once part of a longer row, and some of the fallen ones lie at their base, giving a hint of how awe-inspiring the original layout must once have been. What remains is still spectacular. Further on towards Skibbereen lies Lough Abisdealy, the Lake of the Monster. There have been sightings of something here in past centuries – a gigantic eel or water snake, displaying formidable hoops and coils as it swam across the lake. Despite this, or maybe because of it, reed-fringed Lough Abisdealy is a popular area for birdwatchers.

Castlehaven, to the south of Castletownshend, played its part in the 1601 rebellion, for it was here that six Spanish ships landed more than two thousand men in preparation for the ill-fated Battle of Kinsale, when the English defeated the Irish/Spanish combination. Horse Island (there are several islands of this

Above: The dramatic tall stones at Garranes, not far from Castletownshend. They are the remaining members of a once far longer prehistoric alignment.

name around the coast – you decide which one best deserves first place), with an old burial ground, is just offshore here, separated from the mainland by the intriguingly-named Flea Sound.

Toe Head is an Anglicisation of Ceann Tuaithe, or 'Promontory of the Clan', a name which suits this headland far better. It doesn't get a lot of visitors, and most of the time it's just you and the seabirds and the splendid Atlantic views. An old signal tower, and far earlier promontory forts, keep watch for marauders approaching by sea; donkeys and cattle graze in small fields; bushes and shrubs are bent permanently landward, witness to the prevailing south westerly winds. Ceann Tuaithe has seen many shipwrecks over the years, one of the most recent being that of the *Kowloon Bridge* ore carrier which was driven aground in 1986, remaining visible for several weeks before being firmly and inexorably removed by the sea, which probably took exception to having its pristine shoreline thus disfigured.

Only a short distance away is Lough Hyne, an internationally recognised marine nature reserve. It's actually a semi-marine lake linked to the sea through narrow Barloge Creek. It may well once have been freshwater more than four thousand years ago, before a rise in sea levels joined it with the ocean. A narrow, shallow part of Barloge Creek is known as the rapids, and here the power of the water rushing through at ebb and flood tides is dramatic to see. In other parts, the water can be as deep as 52m. Lough Hyne received the accolade of being designated Europe's very first Marine Nature Reserve in 1981, to protect its extraordinarily rich biodiversity, and scientific research continues here today,

Below: On Toe Head, or Ceann Tuaithe, a grassy lane leads down towards the sea and a fine view of the Stags rocks where many a ship came to grief.

much of it administered through the Zoology Department of University College, Cork.

On one side, modern scientific research, on the other, ancient beliefs. The woods behind Lough Hyne hold a sacred well which has earned a far-reaching reputation over the centuries for curing all kinds of eye ailments. It's quite close to a narrow footpath, but can only be reached by stepping across a stream into a grove of trees. It's pleasant to consider this step as one from the strictly practical world into one of trust and faith. The stone wall built around the well is covered not only with the thick moss which is characteristic of the damp woodlands of West Cork, but also with beads, shells, images, statues, indecipherable notes, pieces of carved wood, rags, rusty pins, jewellery – every kind of token, and each one representing a prayer, a wish, a fervent plea. They may be called holy wells today, but the religion demonstrated in these places is a far older one, deeply rooted in nature and the power of the earth.

Skibbereen, or 'little boat harbour', is a busy market town, but holds, like so many other Irish centres, sad memories of harder times. The Heritage Centre houses a permanent Famine exhibition, and Abbeystrewery graveyard to the west of town, on the banks of the Ilen, may hold as many as ten thousand victims of the Hungry Forties in its mass graves (tragically, we will never know just how many died during those years). In the film *Michael Collins*, Liam Neeson sings the traditional emigrant song, 'Dear Old Skibbereen':

Above: The Rapids at Barloge Creek on Lough Hyne, where at the turn of the tide the rush of water is spectacular.

My son, I loved our native land with energy and pride
Until a blight fell on the land, and sheep and cattle died,
The rents and taxes were to pay, I could not them redeem,
And that's the cruel reason why I left Old Skibbereen.

The *Skibbereen Eagle* newspaper gained international fame in the late nineteenth century when it declared proudly and threateningly that it had 'got its eye both upon Lord Palmerston and on the Emperor of Russia'. Far-off countries might wage war, crowns might be lost in remote kingdoms, but never let readers of the *Eagle* doubt that its editor had his finger on the very pulse of politics. The observation was widely reported in the English press, but it is not known whether the Czar was made officially aware of a beady glance from West Cork!

Above: Flower baskets and a venerable bicycle enhance the sleepy atmosphere of Skibbereen. **Below:** 'And the stately ships go on to their haven under the hill.' Baltimore is the place to be if you love messing about in boats.

Baltimore and the Islands

Baltimore, with its lively quayside and cheerful atmosphere, is totally of the sea, of messing around in boats, of all things maritime. It's been like that for a long time: the area was settled by Celts some two thousand years ago and ever since

sailors and sea-lovers have been drawn here by its superb setting and its relaxed air. This is the very heart of O'Driscoll territory, and regular clan gatherings are held in and around Baltimore, with those who claim kinship coming from all corners of the world to meet and talk and exchange family history.

O'Driscolls notwithstanding, English settlers moved into Baltimore in the early years of the seventeenth century; however, the infamous Sack of Baltimore by Algerian pirates in 1631, in which over a hundred local people were carried off as slaves, somewhat dented the settlers' enthusiasm and they retreated to the comparative safety of Skibbereen further upriver.

Baltimore is also the jumping off place for the islands of Sherkin and Cape Clear, with the *Naomh Ciarán* making the crossing daily. Coming close to departure time, the quays are crowded with backpackers and fishermen, birdwatchers and sightseers, as well as islanders returning from a day's shopping on the mainland. Supplies are stacked ready to load on board as soon as the boat ties up. In rough weather, when the ferry cannot make the crossing to Cape Clear, islanders have to go without or thank their foresight for stocking up in advance, while visitors may have to extend their island adventure for longer than they anticipated.

That's not so likely to happen on Sherkin (from the Irish 'Inis Earcáin'), which lies close to the mainland, a mere few minutes' voyage from Baltimore. It's a small and gently undulating island, no more than three miles long by one and a half wide, with a resident population of about a hundred. Its main industry is the marine station which monitors the flora and fauna of Roaringwater Bay and does sterling service in introducing young people to the wonders of nature. In summer it's popular with families who enjoy the peace and quiet as well as the uncrowded beaches.

From the beach on Sherkin, Cape Clear is clearly visible, lying out at the entrance to Roaringwater Bay, about eight miles from Baltimore. It's both Ireland's southernmost inhabited and southernmost Gaeltacht island, where the native tongue is still everyday speech. According to the Annals of Innisfallen, St Ciarán was born in Cape Clear, in AD 352, which is why the ferry is called after him.

Life on Cape Clear is at the same time extremely laid-back and extremely practical. Niceties like keeping a car in showroom condition are rightly ignored, and some of the most delightful examples of old bangers can be seen bumping up and down the one steeply winding road, known affectionately as the A1. You might see a coat hanger doing service as an aerial, even a teaspoon in the ignition. Baling twine is a perfectly sensible way to keep a bumper secure.

The weather can be wild and windy at any time of the year and the traditional, sturdily-built stone houses huddle into sheltering bushes. Birds blown off course land gratefully on this offshore haven to feed and recover before continuing their interrupted migration. There has been a bird observatory here for over fifty years, and eager birdwatchers throng here in autumn, scanning every tiny garden, every stunted wind-twisted tree for the latest rarity before converging on the pub to swap sightings. Tall tales take on a greater importance on the first weekend in September each year, when the storytelling festival is held, participants from all over the world competing with local experts. Chuck Kruger, a resident islander who founded the festival in 1994, remembers an old fisherman telling him of traditional storytelling nights when one story would cap another into the wee small hours until 'the fella with one eye sat down in the corner' – this is a spine-chilling reference to a long-gone shanachie or storyteller who still, reputedly, made the rounds on dark nights, seeking a place by the fire to tell his own tales.

The past is all around on Cape Clear, with many prehistoric monuments, including a passage tomb, an early church, and a medieval castle. Perhaps most evocative of all are the two standing stones to be found at the eastern end of the island. Originally there were four, but only two now remain upright. One, with

Opposite: This sturdy little stone cottage is built to withstand the fierce storms that can sweep over Cape Clear island without warning.

Below: You're always sure to make new friends along the way. These donkeys at Ceann Tuaithe are more than willing to exchange pleasantries. **Opposite:** This stretch of coastline positively urges you to go paddling, canoeing, exploring rock pools, rediscovering the joys of childhood.

a hole bored right through the centre, has always been known as Cloch na Geallóna, or the 'Trysting Stone', since it is believed to have been used in ages past to seal the vow of betrothal. They were practical about marriage in early Ireland, when the Brehon laws and not Christianity held sway: a couple could marry for a year and a day, and then, if they were not satisfied with the partnership, return after that time and break the vow, with no shame or stain attached to either. If there were children, they went to the mother's clan.

On a wild blustery day, the wind hurls itself at Cape Clear with ferocious force, and knocks the breath out of you. Yet to wander its peaceful lanes on a sunny afternoon, between banks of montbretia and fuchsia, pausing to look out to sea, is to experience the deep down timeless peace that only an island can give. One glance back at the mainland, though, shows the winding road to Mizen beckoning you ever onward.

CHAPTER III

OF SMUGGLERS
AND SHIPWRECKS

THE MIZEN PENINSULA

As chequered and colourful a history as the wildest adventure story. From Spanish galleons to starving emigrants, lobster fisheries to lighthouse builders, this region has known them all.

R oaringwater Bay really marks the beginning of the Mizen peninsula. Just outside Skibbereen on the N71 at Church Cross, a side road down to Cunnamore Quay offers a first view of that splendid stretch of water from an unusual angle. This is where a ferry service runs across to Heir (or Hare, nobody has ever been able to make up their mind) Island, once a busy boatbuilding and lobster fishing centre, but now more of a quiet peaceful backwater – although lobster pots stacked on the quayside at Cunnamore are evidence that the old industry is still operating, albeit on a smaller scale.

The boats made at Heir Island were of a very distinctive type, with a tent-like canvas shelter on the deck to provide some protection from the elements during long fishing trips. The Heir Island fishermen would work the coastline either up as far as the Old Head of Kinsale or down to Castletownbere, staying away a week or more at a time, and coming ashore to sell their catch on quaysides in busy centres of population. Cormac Levis, a maritime researcher from an old West Cork family, has written a book, *Towelsail Yawls*, a detailed record of the lobsterboats of this region.

Pages 82-83: Dunlough Bay near Three Castle Head.
Below: Long Island, the Calves, and, in the background, Cape Clear, seen from Colla, near Schull.

Above: Kilcoe Castle outside Schull, splendidly and accurately restored by actor Jeremy Irons.

Kilcoe Castle stands on the rocky islet of Mannin Beg in Roaringwater Bay, looking out to sea as it has done since the fifteenth century. It's in far better condition than most of its contemporaries though, since it has had the good fortune to be restored by two of the acting profession's aristocracy, husband and wife team Jeremy Irons and Sinéad Cusack, who have had a home nearby for many years. Jeremy, who has written at length on his website about the huge and lengthy (and yes, enormously expensive) restoration task, took endless pains to ensure that Kilcoe would be as true to the original as possible, while still achieving at least some of the comforts (dryness, warmth, stability) that we tend to take for granted today. For the final render, he chose to add ferrous sulphate to the traditional limewash, giving the castle a wonderful almost Tuscan shade of sunlit peach. Of course, this didn't please everyone, particularly those purists who prefer old buildings to look old and decayed, rather than as they would have looked when new-built, but most find it a wonderful sight, and entirely appropriate for the grand backdrop of Roaringwater Bay. It is heartening to see even one of our numerous ruined castles restored with such devoted attention to historical detail. Perhaps others, inspired by Jeremy Irons' achievement, will go and do likewise.

Ballydehob to Schull and Goleen

At the top of the hill approaching the brightly-coloured houses of Ballydehob, a heartstopping panorama opens ahead. This landscape, stretching ahead as far as the eye can see, along a wildly erratic and zigzagging coastline to Schull, Goleen and Crookhaven, is the place most people mean when they say West Cork. There's something about it that catches your heart, ensnares your senses, keeps you coming back for more. Maybe it's the translucent light that gives every gorse

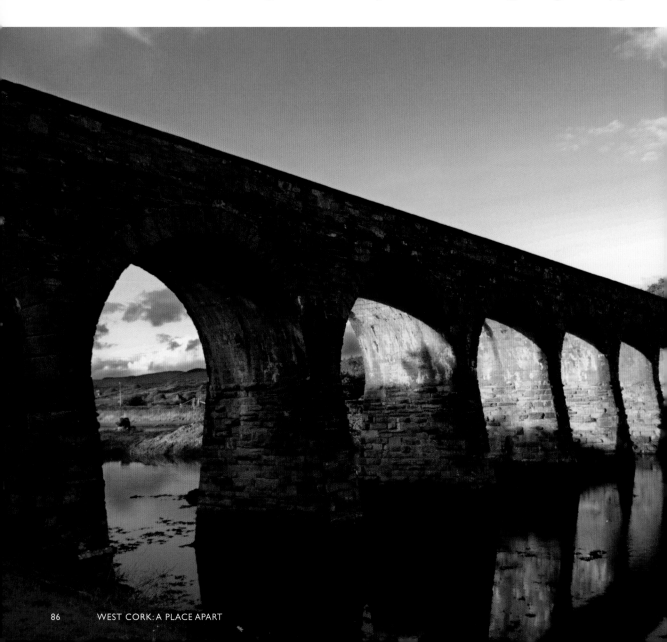

bush, every lichen-covered stone wall, an almost surreal air; maybe it's the way the rocks gradually but insistently take over from fields, thrusting themselves upwards in ever-expanding ranks, tucking casual clumps of heather into their crevices by way of adornment; maybe it's the soporific atmosphere, born of sunlit seas and soft breezes. Tennyson must surely have had this region in mind when he described a land,

in which it seemed always afternoon.

Of course since it's the West Cork most people mean, you couldn't exactly call it undiscovered, hidden. Unless you take the road less travelled, that is, get off the through route marked so clearly and instructively on your map, and wander, as fate intended, along winding byways skirting the sea. You may have to make the occasional three-point turn, retrace your steps now and again; you may well find yourself in a farmyard when you intended quite a different destination; but the sense of discovery will cure forever the tendency to follow the herd.

Ballydehob does look extremely charming, lying peacefully at the head of its very own, infinitesimally small bay of the same name, which opens into the vast parent bay of Roaringwater. The splendid multi-arched railway bridge dominates the village dramatically, although the Skibbereen & Schull Light Tramway (so called, even though it took full-sized trains) is, alas, no more. Those multi-coloured houses, tradition says, were originally so painted that pillars of the local community, returning from serious and lengthy discussion in the local hostelries might each know which one was their own,

Opposite: The splendid twelve-arched bridge, which once carried the West Cork Railway, crosses an inlet of Roaringwater Bay at Ballydehob.

with no fear of entering a neighbour's home by mistake. The more likely truth of it is that painting your property pale yellow, pink, blue or green, is the instinctive expression of a delight in variety and contrast, a deep distrust of the ordinary, the predictable.

There is absolutely no need to take the main road to Schull. Nobody should be in that much of a hurry in West Cork. Instead, turn firmly due south from Ballydehob, pass underneath an arch of the railway bridge, and thread your way through the maze of narrow coastal boreens through little settlements like Foilnamuck and Cappaghglass. The latter hamlet saw much activity in the nineteenth century, when copper mining brought employment and prosperity, but now any signs of former industry are well hidden under the long grasses and twining brambles. The fishing trade too, once a valuable source of income for hundreds of families on this stretch of coast, is today barely evident. The sleepy port of Rossbrin, where once the copper ore was shipped to England, has the old O'Mahony castle still standing proudly, reminder of a time when these lords controlled the rich fishing waters and extracted dues and payments from visiting French or Spanish boats.

They valued learning too – or at least one of them did. Medieval Fineen The Scholar (not on any account to be confused with the much later and much more inclined to wander, Fineen The Rover), amongst other academic activities found time to translate Sir John Mandeville's *Travels in the Holy Land* from English into Irish. Praiseworthy though this undoubtedly seems to us today, you can't help wondering if the rest of his lordly family looked askance at one of their number who, strangely, preferred curling up with quill and parchment instead of going out attacking neighbouring chieftains, looting and pillaging, or generally causing a rumpus, like any normal nobleman.

Horse, Castle, and Long Islands lie close to the shore here, their grassy slopes tempting you out across the glittering water to play at Robinson Crusoe; but getting to them would require going on to the harbour at Schull, unless, of course, you thought far enough ahead to strap a boat to the roof of your car. Travelling throughout West Cork, the desirability of owning your own boat returns again and again until it becomes an obsession. In fact, living down here would make a boat more of a practical necessity than a luxury, enabling miles of twisting roads to be bypassed on the way to collect the papers or do the shopping. There's something very satisfying in crossing a creek for the bread.

Rowing out to the Fastnet lighthouse would be a bit more of a challenge. Up to a few decades ago there were still elderly men living around here who claimed to have transported all the stone out to the Fastnet Rock in their rowboats during the building works between 1899 and 1904, being paid two shillings and sixpence (about 12c) a day for the job. It's a nice idea, but not really practicable, given the size of the massive blocks of Cornish granite, and in fact the truth of the story is that a specially commissioned small steamer was used for this heavy work. It is quite likely, though, that the locals did row out each day to assist with the construction work.

It's the highest lighthouse in Ireland – a hundred and eight feet (about 3300cm) high at low tide, ninety-eight (2987cm) at the full, in case anyone ever asks you – and is actually the second structure on the rock. The first one, built in 1853, simply wasn't strong enough to withstand the appalling weather conditions that can occur here. Yachtsmen who participate in the famed Fastnet Race, held every four years, have good cause to know those conditions: the storm which blew up during the 1979 event resulted in the deaths of no fewer than fifteen competitors. The Fastnet Rock is the most southerly point in the

country, known in earlier, less fortunate times as 'Ireland's Teardrop', since it was the last glimpse of their native land that tearful passengers saw as the emigrant ships bore them far to the west and a new way of life.

There's another O'Mahony stronghold a few miles on, at Ardintenant. White Castle (probably so named because Black Castle is further along the coast again) is a little unusual, being set, not overlooking the water, but well back in a sheltered little valley with a track leading down to the water. Though hardly in the optimum position for keeping an eye on marauding fishermen or pirates, its residents might well have had the last laugh on wild winter nights when gales and high seas were battering their more strategically-located neighbours.

And so you come round by Coosheen to Schull. That's if all the other tiny side roads pointing to the shoreline, ending maybe at a little slipway, maybe just on a deserted beach, are firmly ignored. You could do worse than spend the whole day exploring those little links between mainland and water. But Schull is waiting. Before you reach the town, though, turn up the steep road to Mount Gabriel and see the whole of West Cork laid out below you in all its incredible beauty. 'That view would twist the heart in you,' a lonely expatriate told me amid the roaring traffic of New York.

Of all the villages in West Cork, Schull is probably the best known and the most discovered. Once a little fishing port, its narrow main street was never meant for the gridlock of cars that descends upon it day in, day out, in season. The fine natural harbour is thronged with gleaming craft, while shops sell fashionable striped sweaters and designer deck-shoes as well as the basic necessities. On a fine day, chairs and tables spill out of cafés and pubs on to the pavement and threading your way from one end of the street to the other can take quite a while. It's all great fun, if more reminiscent of Cannes than Cork. But again, if crowds aren't your thing, take to the coastal lanes and boreens, and you'll have the endless seas and skies and soaring seabirds all to yourself.

Every turn, every corner brings something new – the rich orange of montbretia clashing with the vivid pink of fuchsia, an old stone wall splashed with the vivid orange of lichens, a prosperous whitewashed farmhouse with the original tiny stone cottage that probably reared several generations now relegated to the indignity of henhouse or toolshed, a stream tumbling down to a pebbly beach no bigger than a backyard, an old green lane winding up a hillside, an ancient graveyard with long grasses waving around the tilting headstones.

On Toormore Bay is Black Castle, also known as Leamcon, or 'the hound's leap', another stronghold of the many-branched O'Mahony clan, which passed into the hands of Sir William Hull, an English settler loyal to the Crown, in the

Above: The Fastnet lighthouse, iconic image of the West Cork coastline and last glimpse of Ireland for many emigrants over the centuries.

seventeenth century. Sir William built a fine mansion on the mainland behind Black Castle, but nothing remains of that original house today, while Black Castle, restored and renovated, still stands firm, staring out to sea from its separated headland, reached by a narrow bridge. For the full story of what happened to Sir William's home (and indeed his business interests in this region), you'll have to wait till we get to Crookhaven.

The number of megalithic tombs, standing stones, and other echoes of an ancient past on this stretch of coastline can't even be estimated. There are two close to the townland of Altar, near Toormore, one which you can look at easily since it's close to the road, the other more difficult to locate on a high ridge of rock. It's certain, however, that those marked on the map are only a sample of the number still waiting to be rediscovered. Even if you go looking for a specific, marked site, you might not find it – but you'll certainly find something else to console you, be it a tiny, jewel-bright orchid half-hidden in the grass, or a tumbling stream where you can paddle and be six years old again.

Beyond Goleen the road squeezes itself between high rocky slopes on one side – where you might see a peregrine perch – and a sheer drop to the sea on the other, while across the water, Crookhaven comes into view out at the end

of its peninsula. Rock Island is just off the road a short distance outside Goleen; there were lobster fisheries here for many years, supplying the French market. Further on, sharp eyes will spot the remains of an old stone quarry on the cliffs where chutes carried the material down to boats which transported it to Wales for roadbuilding. It's one of those ironies of trading that Cornish granite should be shipped to West Cork with great effort for building a lighthouse, while stone from Goleen quarry, with similar effort, went the other way; but it has ever been thus.

There is an alternative route out of Goleen, albeit more challenging, which twists right up over the hills. The spectacular bird's-eye view it offers over the long inlet and Crookhaven slumbering in the sunshine, makes it worth the effort. Both roads meet up shortly before the head of the creek and the signpost where you go one way for Crookhaven and the other for Barley Cove and Mizen Head. Just before the head of the creek, there is another reminder of our ancient, uncomprehended past: a curious layout of tall rocks, fully visible only at low tide, which may well be a prehistoric stone row. Often a gull or two is perching on it, bringing the past and the present into momentary harmony. Hidden deep in the bracken-drowned slopes above are two huge megalithic tombs, but they're quite a way up and difficult to find without a detailed map and sometimes even with one. They're in a wonderful setting, though, gazing out over the bay below and the vast Atlantic beyond.

Crookhaven

Crookhaven lies about as far down in south-west Cork as you can go without falling into the sea, tucked snugly on the sheltered side of a narrow neck of land which creates a deep inlet. Outside high season, when you can't move for four-wheel-drives, it's the very epitome of a sleepy fishing village. Brightly-coloured boats bob at anchor; pastel-coloured cottages slumber in the sunshine along the sloping street. A pub spills tables and chairs out on to the quayside among the drying fishing nets, a small shop sells groceries and postcards as well as shrimping nets, buckets and spades. It looks as though nothing ever has or ever could happen to disturb its peace.

Yet Crookhaven has as chequered and colourful a history as the wildest adventure story. Smuggling and shipwrecks, burnings and battles, East India merchantmen and Spanish galleons, lobsters, pilchards, traders, businessmen, soldiers, spies and starving emigrants – it has known them all. This tiny settlement even played a major role in the development of world communications, and at one time was a vital link between Wall Street and London.

The principal reasons for Crookhaven's enduring importance from early times are threefold: firstly, its extensive, deep, safe harbour, almost a mile in length, protected from all but the most unusual winds; secondly, that harbour's strategic location at one of the last landfall points on the Irish coast, for either the southern route to Spain, Portugal and Africa, or the western route for the New World; and thirdly, the exceptionally rich fishing grounds in the surrounding waters.

It is probable that Greek and Phoenician traders visited this coastline in ancient times. By the twelfth century, there was a church here, dedicated to St Molaga – perhaps the same saint who gave his name to the abbey of Timoleague (Tigh Molaga) further back along the coast towards Cork. In the sixteenth century, when England was making determined attempts to subdue her troublesome neighbour, she kept a very sharp eye on this outlying harbour, fully aware of the dangers to be feared from unfriendly countries wishing to ally themselves with

Opposite: Lace-fringed waves sweeping in to the golden sands of Barley Cove.

The long headland of
Crookhaven, the deeply-
indented southern side facing
the wild Atlantic, while on the
northern side a long and
sheltered bay provides ideal
mooring for yachts and
pleasure boats.

the Irish rebels. It would be all too easy for a French or Spanish fighting ship to slip into Crookhaven unnoticed. In 1601, just prior to the fateful Battle of Kinsale, there were constant rumours of Spanish galleons arriving at or sailing close by Crookhaven. In September of that year, Sir George Carew wrote urgently to the Privy Council:

> There arrived at Crookehaven one Captain Love who in a small pinnace recovered this coast and from thence overland came unto me. Before this can come into your hands, it is very probable that the Spaniards will make their descent in Ireland. He saw the fleet (full of land men and ensigns) stand to the northward and they are bound for this realm. He reports that most of the Irish that are in Spain are in the fleet…

In early December, a terse message to the Queen's representative spoke of 'Spanish ships arrived at Crookhaven', but, tantalisingly, there are no further details on the records to confirm this. Tradition has it, however, that a Spanish ship was wrecked at Galley Cove, a rocky bay a mile or so back from the village on the seaward side of the peninsula. Shipwrecks have been an inevitable part of life here throughout history, due to the rough waters and savage rocks – hard to believe when you are on the quiet, landward side, but very much there, nevertheless. One such wreck was that of the *Barbara*, out of Berehaven, which sank with a cargo of spirits in the harbour in 1829. A hundred and forty years later, this writer's father recovered several bottles of brandy while diving on the wreck, and claimed that the contents were still drinkable.

Despite its tiny size, Crookhaven has a long history as a trading port because of its strategic position. In the seventeenth century it was listed along with larger harbours like Cork, Waterford and Limerick, as being one of the principal exporters of wool, hides, yarn, hogshead staves and pipestaves. There is evidence of exotic items being imported in return, including ginger and other spices, as well as silks. In later centuries, large quantities of butter, oats, wheat and pork were exported, with timber and coal being occasionally imported. Until relatively modern times, overland communications between Crookhaven and the rest of Ireland were extremely difficult, and goods were transported onwards by coastal vessels. Partly because of this high trading profile, but also because the harbour came to be much used by the English navy and East India merchant ships as a useful stopping point on longer voyages, this isolated little village boasted customs and excise, coastguards and a police barracks, all established by

Opposite: Dawn over Crookhaven, and the sun, rising through the clouds, touches the still water with gold.

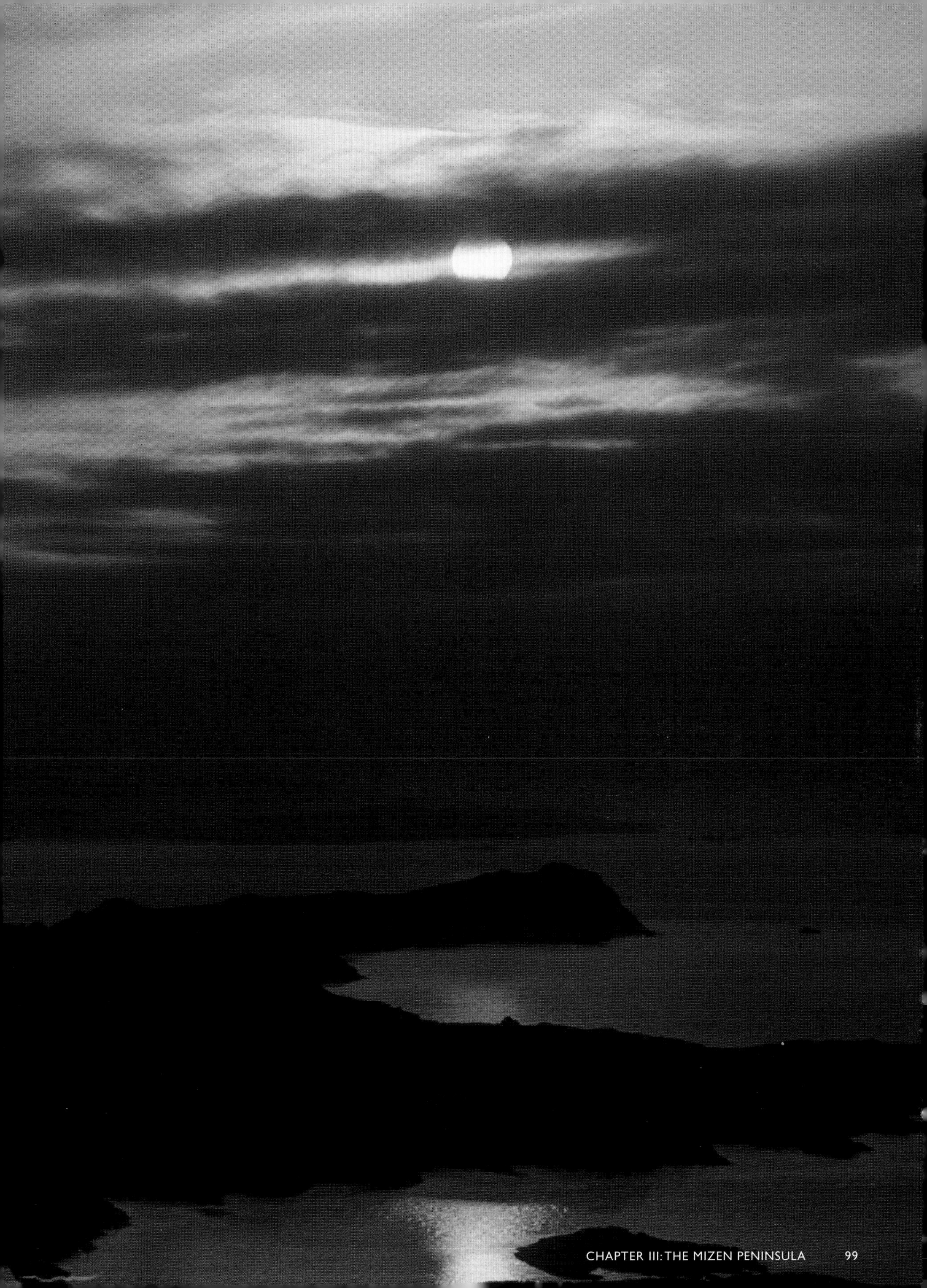

the English government to protect fishing activities and prevent smuggling, as well as watching for potential coastal invasion or the infiltration of enemy spies.

Despite the best efforts of authority, it is likely that a good deal of smuggling did go on. There are several deep caves hidden under Streek Head which forms the tip of the Crookhaven peninsula, and tradition has it that these were used by illegal traders to store their precious cargoes of lace and old brandy. At a time when English strictures forbade the export of native wool, local people delighted too in finding ingenious ways to get fleeces out to the waiting markets in Europe. One popular trick was to pack the wool tightly in butter casks, sealing it with a layer of the official product so that if opened, it would appear to be full of butter. And on moonless nights, there would be hushed voices in quiet inlets from whence small boats would make their way to ships waiting out at sea. After such night-time activity, the next morning might show telltale scraps of wool caught on thorn bushes, but seldom were the smugglers caught.

Fishing and the export of fish have always been important here. In the sixteenth century, Sir William Hull, an English tenant of the Earl of Cork, developed an industry across the harbour from the village. In his 'pilchard palace', fish was salted or smoked and then barrelled for export. It gave useful employment to many people in the surrounding area, but this did not stop them rising against Sir William during the 1641 rebellion, attacking his household, burning his property to the ground, and carrying off all his goods. The aggrieved Sir William immediately wrote to the English Crown, listing in detail everything he had lost with a careful valuation of each item, including 'all the fishing sellers [cellars] which cost above £3,500'. In later years, merchants from Brittany sailed across regularly to bargain with local fishermen for lobster, crawfish, sea urchins, periwinkles and salmon with which to furnish French dining tables.

In 1659, Crookhaven had just 36 inhabitants. By 1837, the population had expanded to 424 – a large number for such a small area. By this time communications had been improved by the making of the Skibbereen–Crookhaven road during the famine of 1822-23, both as a relief measure and as a public work. The population of Crookhaven may have felt that times were improving. Then came 1847 and a far more terrible famine than anyone could have imagined.

The little settlement was cruelly hit. There were two soup kitchens set up there in 1847, an indication of the relief needed. Of ninety-one children on the school roll in 1846, only eight remained in March 1847. Now the position of

Opposite: Brow Head was once the site of a thriving coppermining industry, now only the ruined cottages of the miners and officials bear witness to the past.

the safe harbour as the last landfall on the Irish coast became something of a blessing. Ships pausing before the Atlantic crossing took on large numbers of desperate and starving emigrants who had not the means to get to Cork.

In the 1850s and 60s there was much activity around the copper mines which were opened on Streek and Brow Heads by speculators. Copper has been mined in this part of West Cork on a small scale since prehistoric times, and although the Crookhaven mines never produced very much, they would have given welcome employment to many before they closed in the 1860s. Today, evidence of their presence can still be seen on Brow Head in the ruined cottages of former mine workers, or even in the green-streaked stones which can be picked up everywhere. The mine shafts on Brow Head were actually driven into the rocks down at water level, turning and going right out under the sea where the miners chipped away to extract the valuable ore, which was then lifted up to the top of the cliff by cable. It would be a curious experience to be down there beneath the ocean, listening to the dull roar overhead; Wilkie Collins described just such a visit to a mine in Cornwall in the 1850s:

After listening for a few moments, a distant, unearthly noise becomes faintly audible –
a long, low, mysterious moaning … The miner tells us that what we hear is the sound
of the surf lashing the rocks a hundred and twenty feet above us … Just over our heads
we observe a wooden plug of the thickness of a man's leg; there is a hole here, and the
plug is all that we have to keep out the sea.
(Rambles Beyond Railways)

The next two people to influence Crookhaven's history were also to make vital use of Brow Head. Julius Reuter, who had built up his reputation as a provider of news stories from across the world, decided to set up a signal station here in 1863 from which information newly arrived from America could be transmitted to Cork by telegraph wire and thence to London. A signal tower dating from Napoleonic times was utilised as lookout point, and his staff rowed out to meet the steamers as they arrived from their Atlantic crossing to retrieve canisters tossed overboard containing despatches from Reuter's staff. It was thus that the latest news from the American Civil War was received in London. Since it got to Cork first, however, the *Cork Examiner* was often able to publish a 'scoop' in advance of the London *Times* – a feat which delighted its editors inordinately. Mail came by this watery route too; in fact, there were once plans to extend the railway from Ballydehob as far as Crookhaven to make the service even speedier, but it came to nothing. A pity indeed, since a railway winding along that scenic coast would be worth a fortune in tourism terms today.

After the telegraph, came the turn of radio. Guglielmo Marconi, whose mother was Irish, and who had married a daughter of the Earl of Inchiquin, decided that Crookhaven would be an excellent site for a radio station which would transfer messages from America to England. He accordingly set this up in 1901 in an old police barracks in the village, later moving it to Brow Head, close to the old signal tower used by Reuter. Arthur Nottage from Derbyshire was the first manager of Marconi's station; he grew to love the place and when he retired, opened a small pub in the village. His name can still be seen above the door, although 'Daddy Nottage', as he was affectionately known, has long since passed on.

The little church of St Brendan, which stands on a grassy knoll above the village, dates from the 1700s, but probably replaces earlier buildings. In its peaceful graveyard the grass waves long and tall around ancient stones which record losses at sea, untimely drownings, or the quiet end of a well-run life. This church and graveyard featured in a 1950s film, *I Thank A Fool*, starring Susan Hayward, and in O'Sullivan's pub on the quayside, faded black-and-white stills from the film (in which all the villagers delightedly appeared as extras) are still displayed with pride.

Mizen Head and Dunmanus Bay

The vast golden sands at Barley Cove are a spectacular sight, backed by high sand dunes with a river running through and down to the shore from Lissagriffin Lake. The lake itself, crossed by a causeway, is renowned for turning up rare migrant birds, while the ruins of a former chapel and graveyard look down from the hill above, reminders that the population here was once far larger. All the way out to Mizen, though, are similar reminders, clusters of little houses where voices once called and hands tilled fields, now settling back into the quiet landscape.

Mizen Head, the most south-westerly point in Ireland, 'next parish, America', although beautiful at any time, is actually seen at its dramatic best on a wild, blustery day when the relentless waves far below tear at the cliffs and send yellow foam flying up, even over the headland, while the hoarse-calling choughs toss

Opposite: The Napoleonic watch tower on Brow Head, utilised by both Reuter and Marconi to communicate with the other side of the Atlantic.

The seas crash on rugged cliffs at Mizen Head, Ireland's most south-westerly point. In the distance, Sheep Head, and, further back, the Kerry mountains can be seen.

and tumble with delight in the updraught. The lighthouse – or more accurately the fog signal station – is on a separate, steep-sided island, with a dizzying bridge linking the two. It was built to mitigate in some measure the appalling number of shipwrecks on this dangerous stretch of coastline. Today, although the signal is automated, the history of its construction and the life of those who maintained it is displayed in a permanent exhibition complete with original early photographs and records, while up on the main headland is an extended interpretative centre.

Coming back from Mizen, a narrow road to the left goes as far as a tiny slipway on Dunlough Bay and stops with a sigh of relief. This is as far as it's going to take you, so it's time to get the boots on. The walk out to Three Castle Head will take a good fifteen or twenty minutes, but you know those Michelin green guidebooks which rate attractions as worth a stop, a detour, or, just occasionally, a special trip? Three Castle Head is worth everything and more. You hike through long grass, push past gorse bushes glittering with dewy spiders' webs, catch your clothes on treacherous brambles, climb crumbling stone walls, and all the while wonder where you're going and why you set out at all. Then you come over a little rise and the splendour of the sight takes your breath away.

Three castles in one, really, since the two outlying towers are part of the layout of central Dunlough Castle. Dunlough has the distinction of being mentioned

in the Annals of Innisfallen, which gives the date of its construction as 1217. It is set in a sheltered little valley behind the headland, but close enough to keep a sharp eye on Dunlough Bay below; doubtless, lookouts were posted constantly on the cliffs to give advance warning of visitors, welcome or otherwise (it was usually otherwise). It is an experience like no other to stand on this remote headland, look at those crumbling walls, and imagine the bustle, the noise, the constant coming and going, the sheer numbers of servants and helpers and suppliers and hewers of wood and drawers of water required to maintain such an establishment at a time when each large castle was a community, a virtual town in itself. It is tempting, too, to draw Arthurian comparisons, imagine mysterious denizens of the lake rising to command a young prince to seek his destiny.

Northside of the Mizen, the road in towards Durrus along the sweep of Dunmanus Bay passes the gaunt finger of ruined Dunbeacon, the remains of Durode copper mines, and stunning Dunmanus Castle. Near Durrus, two ancient sites beckon: the two remaining members of an earlier, more complete stone row are easily located next to a farmhouse driveway; but the site to which they point, on a hill at the other side of the minor road, is reachable only with a bit of effort, ducking under a wire fence or two, hiking a steep slope, clambering over a ditch. When Dunbeacon stone circle is finally gained, however, you'll have it to yourself – apart from whatever spirits may guard its leaning grey warriors. Climb the last few feet to the top of the hill and see Dunmanus Bay stretched out below. Time it for sunset if you can. Sunrise would be even better.

Sheep's Head

Coming in along Dunmanus Bay, the long, quiet length of Sheep's Head to the north has been visible all the way. Where the Mizen Peninsula is well discovered, Sheep's Head is still relatively unknown. Locals claim that the Gulf Stream is responsible for the mild climate which often brings daffodils out in early January at Kilcrohane while the rest of the country is only waking up. Ahakista, slumbering amid luxuriant hedges of escallonia, a shrub that loves the salt air, with fuchsia shaking its crimson bells over the roadway, induces a sense of relaxation akin to drowsiness. It's dangerously easy to call at the inn here for a break in the driving and simply sit there for the rest of the day, gazing out into the old-world gardens by the shore. After all, the self-indulgence can be

Opposite: Three Castle Head, on its remote promontory between Mizen and Dunmanus, is one of the most spectacular settings on the south west coast.

combated later with an energetic walk.

While England has the provision of well-marked, strictly-monitored footpaths polished to a fine art by this time, we've never been great ones for holding the hands of hikers in this country. Let them sort it out for themselves, was the casual approach in times past, and sure, if they get lost, they won't go far. Times are changing, though. The Sheep's Head Way is one of the most recently created waymarked walks, and has become extremely popular, probably due to its pleasant combination of low hills and splendid cliff coastline. It runs along a mix of paths, tracks and quiet roads, and is easy going even for those who wouldn't consider themselves seasoned ramblers.

On foot, the Sheep's Head Way makes a full circuit of the peninsula; by car, it is possible to get out as far as Tooreen to enjoy the views, but the road ends there, folding its arms and refusing to go further. It's necessary to retrace your steps along the swooping track as far as Ballyroon and Letter West before finding a left turn across to the north side of Sheep's Head. This is the place to leave the car, and do some vigorous walking before returning, full of healthy virtue, to complete the journey to Bantry with a pleasant anticipation of well-earned rest and sustenance.

Opposite: Dunmanus Bay sweeps inland almost to Durrus, with Sheep's Head on its northern shore.
Above: The single remaining wall of Dunbeacon Castle stands gaunt and watchful over Dunmanus Bay at sunset.

CHAPTER IV

AT THE WORLD'S END

THE BEARA PENINSULA

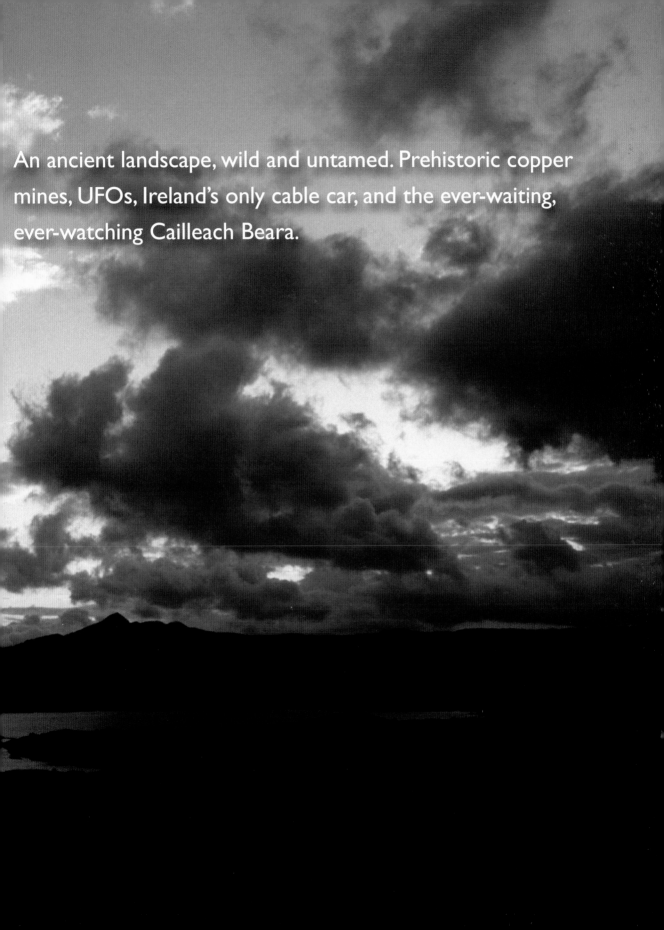

An ancient landscape, wild and untamed. Prehistoric copper mines, UFOs, Ireland's only cable car, and the ever-waiting, ever-watching Cailleach Beara.

The best way to get a really spectacular bird's-eye view of this entire region is from the top of Vaughan's Pass, reached on a side road just before Bantry: the town itself, scattered along the shoreline like a child's forgotten playthings, gracious Bantry House dwarfed to the dimensions of an antique toy, Whiddy Island drowsing in the sunshine, vast Bantry Bay that has played host to some of the world's largest ships, and beyond that, the long stretch of Beara with Hungry Hill looming in solitary splendour between the Caha and the Slieve Miskish ranges. An ancient landscape, relatively wild and untamed, with ever-changing skies above, it's quieter than Mizen and far less discovered than the well-worn Ring of Kerry. You could drive the Ring of Beara in a day if you really wanted – it's not more than 140km – but a peaceful few days wandering would be far more in keeping with the spirit of the place. Leave the car and walk parts of the Beara Way, following tracks along sea cliffs and over the hillsides, or seizing the unique experience of a cable car crossing to Dursey Island.

Pages 110-111: Clouds gather at sunset over the Beara peninsula. **Below:** Old field patterns on the Beara peninsula are testimony to the struggle for survival in the crowded countryside of pre-Famine Ireland.

Beara is sparsely populated, yet visitors have been coming here in great numbers since the eighteenth century at least, to admire the scenery or study local conditions. The construction of reasonable roads and the arrival of the railway increased those numbers vastly, and a visit by the Prince of Wales, afterwards Edward VII, in 1858, put the peninsula well and truly on the map.

The very large number of archaeological remains on the peninsula indicates continuous human activity here from 3000 or 4000 BC. Ancient field systems and walls that predate the covering of the landscape with bog have been found, and more than fifty prehistoric cairns, the largest of which is at Dereenacarrin, between Glengarriff and Castletownbere. Ogham stones, with their cryptic carved lines, wedge graves commemorating once-great figures, stone circles and medieval church sites are scattered everywhere. Wolves and eagles were still plentiful here in 1700 when Bishop Dive Downes visited; today a project is in operation to bring back the sea eagle, with young chicks donated from Norway's ample stock. It's quite a sight to see one of these enormous birds floating majestically overhead on that vast wingspan, as our ancestors must have done.

The legend is that Eoghan Mór, a second-century king of Munster, was driven out of Ireland by Conn of the Hundred Battles. He married Beara, daughter of a Spanish king, and, returning to claim his territory, landed on a peninsula which he named in honour of his wife. Eoghan and Conn gave their names to two later tribal powers – the Eoghanacht who ruled Munster, and the Connachta who gave their name to Connacht. When the O'Sullivans were driven south west by the arriving Anglo-Normans in the twelfth century, they took over from the Eoghanacht. A later leader of the clan, who somewhat retraced his ancestors' steps, was Donal Cam O'Sullivan Beare, who after the disastrous (for Ireland) Battle of Kinsale in 1601, and subsequent siege of Dunboy by the English troops in 1602, barely escaped to make the legendary trek northwards to Leitrim with a thousand followers in the depths of winter. Only thirty-five survived to reach safety. It is in remembrance of that march that the Beara–Breifne long-distance footpath was established.

Copper mines dating from 1500 BC have been found here, also bronze artefacts. Since copper must be blended with tin to create bronze, this indicates early trading at least between Beara and Cornwall (the nearest source of tin), if not further afield.

Maritime tradition stretches from early Vikings in their longships to the British Atlantic Fleet, which used these safe natural harbours right up to the eve of

Whiddy Island in the foreground, overlooking Bantry Bay towards Ballylickey and the road to Glengarriff.

World War II. Today, gaining a living from the sea is still very much part of everyday life, as can be seen from the mussel rafts decorating the sparkling waters.

Bantry

This is a lively, friendly town, with a statue of St Brendan the Navigator welcoming those who enter. On market day he towers above the colourful stalls and crowds, tolerantly watching the goings on. Wolfe Tone Square commemorates the young Irishman who attempted, but failed, to overthrow British rule in 1798 with the help of a French invasion force. The town is a maze of narrow, winding streets, manifestly designed in quieter times for pedestrians, with the occasional carriage or long-distance diligence, not an endless stream of private cars.

The railway came in 1881, first terminating some way back from the centre, but later extended right down to the pier, so that both freight and passengers could make the connection to the Bantry Steamship Company whose boats plied up and down between Bantry, Glengarriff, Adrigole and Castletownbere. And, of course, there was plenty of traffic in the opposite direction too, bringing people and goods up to Cork. It was, as such regional lines are, a lifeline for the Beara Peninsula until the last train ran in 1961. This

is another part of West Cork where there is strong feeling that the railway should return, thus easing pressure on narrow roads never meant for the current volume of traffic, and at the same time decreasing our consumption of expensive fuel resources.

Bantry House stands just on the Cork side of the town, on an eminence overlooking the bay. Built in the mid-eighteenth century, it was originally called Blackrock House. Its owner, Richard White, was ennobled by a grateful British government for the part he played in deflecting the attempted 1798 French invasion, and eventually became the first Earl of Bantry. Much extended in Victorian times, today Bantry House is a remarkably fine example of an Irish country residence, still within the same family, and still with many of the furniture, tapestries, and objets d'art collected over the centuries to be seen in its rooms. It played its part in national affairs, being used as a hospital during the Irish Civil War in 1922, and being occupied by the Second Cyclist Squadron of the Irish Army during World War II. Plaques on the north wall of the house are a sad commemoration of members of the Royal Canadian Air Force who died when their plane crashed off the Fastnet Rock during the war. Fascinatingly,

Opposite: The statue of St Brendan the Navigator stands high above the market place in Bantry town. **Above:** Gracious Bantry House still preserves the ambience of yesteryear.

archaeological work carried out by the University of Ulster in 2001 found evidence of both a medieval Gaelic village and a seventeenth-century English fishing village under the west lawn. There is surely an epic novel in the making here: original inhabitants driven out by colonists; colonial village, in turn, forced to move, lock, stock and cottage, to permit the building of a stately home.

Since 1947, Bantry House has been open to the public, a sensible move by the family to encourage tourism to the area, and it also hosts the West Cork Chamber Music Festival each summer, one of the most delightful settings imaginable for such events. The gardens are as gracious as the house, beautifully laid out, with the famous Hundred Steps rising from the Italianate garden with its ancient wisteria circle surrounding a fountain. Make the climb to the top of the steps and you are rewarded with stunning views over the very roof of the house to Bantry Bay and the Caha mountains beyond.

Whiddy Island is a small, green and peaceful place, no more than 5km long and 2.5km wide, with scattered farmhouses and cottages. You can reach it by ferry from the pier at Bantry in ten or fifteen minutes. It may well have been settled since prehistoric times: the earliest surviving records show that there were at least two monasteries and a priory here around AD 500 – ideal pickings for the

roaming Vikings who called it Holy Island, and doubtless popped in unheralded and uninvited for a cup of tea (or a silver chalice) on more than one occasion. Reenananig Castle was built by the O'Sullivans to keep their grip on trade in and out of the harbour, and the ruins still stand. In the eighteenth century it was home to a prosperous pilchard fishing industry. After the failed French invasion in 1798, the English built gun batteries here to guard against any similar future attempts: you can still see their remains today, but they've settled very peacefully into the bracken and grass and quite forgotten their warlike origins. The Famine hit Whiddy hard, and Lord Bantry's introduction of deer farming made things worse. It wasn't a particularly good idea to object, though; many who did were hanged at a site known to this day as Gallows Hill.

Even the Americans took an interest in Whiddy, building a seaplane base at its eastern end in 1918 to keep an eye on German submarines and shipping. You can just about locate it today by means of a small fountain known as the Cup and Saucer, built by the servicemen posted here. It must have been a stirring sight for the folk of Whiddy and Bantry to see those planes with their massive floats taking off and landing.

Whiddy also enshrines the memory of what is probably Ireland's worst

Above: Glengarriff harbour, looking out towards Garinish Island.
Opposite: Looking down on Bantry Bay from Vaughan's Pass.

Opposite: Garinish or Ilnacullen
Island just offshore at Glengarriff,
was transformed into an Italian
garden by Anna Bryce
in the 1920s.

maritime disaster. The opening of a massive oil terminal in 1971 brought a much-needed boost to the region, which had languished since the closure of the railway. The giant storage tanks were discreetly sited on the seaward side – they are still barely visible even if you drive right up to the crest of Vaughan's Pass. But in January 1979, as the French supertanker *Betelgeuse* was discharging 220,000 tonnes of fuel oil, there was a huge explosion, which covered the entire terminal in burning oil. At least fifty people died. A monument in the graveyard on the mainland nearby commemorates the tragedy and it is marked each year on the fatal date by those from near and far who lost loved ones. Today, after a long hiatus, the economic effects of which were keenly felt in Bantry, the oil terminal is working once more, with up to forty ships berthing every year.

Not far beyond Ballylickey, where the road crosses the Coomhola river tumbling down from the hills, you can turn right and explore the Coomhola Pass, which climbs dramatically up and over the mountains before coming down into Kerry on the other side. Near the county bounds at the summit is Gowlane bridge, the traditional starting point for those taking the old footway over the hills into Gougane Barra, as many do on Pattern Sunday in late September.

But not only healthy hikers are to be seen… This is, after all, officially Ireland's most active region for unexplained strange objects in the sky. According to the Irish Centre for UFO Studies, of some 120 sightings in the West Cork region since around 1990, some 35 have been in the Coomhola area. Some say it has to do with the ley lines that crisscross here, while others take the practical view that since everybody else loves West Cork, why not extra-terrestrials too? The sightings have been taken seriously enough to feature in the ITV programme 'We Are Not Alone'. Perhaps a good place to don a warm sweater, sit on a rock and wait peacefully and silently until midnight when a full moon will pour its radiance on anything that might turn up. Then again, perhaps not.

Glengarriff

The coast road to Glengarriff gives wonderful views out over the bay. This is relatively bare and open countryside, with only the occasional stunted thorn tree leaning well away from the prevailing wind, but once you start dropping down towards the harbour of Glengarriff, the landscape changes dramatically, with lush greenery, magnificent trees and a general abundance of vegetation stating, in no uncertain terms, that the Gulf Stream's beneficent warmth can't be

far away. The same warm waters benefit much of this coastline, giving it a distinctly Mediterranean feel. Temperatures rarely drop below freezing here, and you can see evidence of that in the flourishing tree and shrub species that would have difficulty surviving in less Utopian surroundings. There is even a bamboo park, with magnificent specimens you would expect to find more in the tropics than West Cork.

The name Glengarriff is derived from the Irish, Gleann Garbh, which translates as 'the rough or rugged glen'. It's a special place, with an air of timelessness that is most seductive. Even the sun seems to set later here, but that's hardly surprising, since this part of West Cork is quite a bit away from Greenwich and its authoritative mean time. Back before railways necessitated clockwatching, we kept our own time down here.

Everybody puts Glengarriff on their itinerary. William Makepeace Thackeray (author of, among other best-sellers of their day, *Barry Lyndon* and *Vanity Fair*), came here by 'two-horse car' in 1842, putting up at the Eccles, and was quite evidently enchanted:

What sends picturesque tourists to the Rhine and Saxon Switzerland? Within five miles round the pretty inn of Glengarriff there is a country of which no pen can give an idea … A beautiful bay stretches out before the house, the full tide washing the thorn trees; mountains rise on either side of the little bay, and there is an island with a castle in it, in the midst …

Unfortunately, the endemic heavy rain which, to be fair, contributes in no small part to the luxuriance and greenery, rather cast a damper on his explorations, but happily the Eccles hotel allowed him to dry 'the only suit of clothes I had by the kitchen fire.' Given the traditional relaxed hospitality of Irish hotels, it would probably perform the same kind office for any visitor today, although the original building is now considerably extended and improved from Thackeray's day. The scenery, however, is pretty much as he would have seen it over a century and a half ago, although many of the old estates belonging to the landed gentry are now crumbling, their iron gates padlocked and overgrown with brambles.

There is another, unexpected bit of the Mediterranean to be found here. Even if it escapes your mind, the boatmen and their handwritten signs will remind you that Glengarriff pier is where you embark for Garinish Island (its proper name,

Above: A traditional whitewashed farmhouse near Glengarriff is totally at home in its natural surroundings.
Opposite: The signs of old lazybeds, or ridge and furrow, are very evident in this little lost field between Glengarriff and Adrigole.

The Glengarriff river sweeps through lush woodlands with wild flowers abundant on its banks.

Ilnacullen, or 'the Island of Holly', being almost entirely forgotten) and its legendary Italian gardens. These were created in the 1920s by Anna Bryce, then owner of the island, and Harold Peto, an architect and garden designer. On her death, Bryce generously left the island and its gardens to the Irish nation, so that they could be enjoyed by everyone and not just the few. That the many rare shrubs and trees have thrived ever since is a tribute to the unique blend of climatic conditions to be found here. The place is enchanting. There are water features, winding pathways, stone archways, fountains, and lawns surrounded by rustling trees, all on one tiny island in the middle of a bay. Azaleas and rhododendrons in spring give way to a blaze of colour in summer, followed in turn by splendid heathers and autumn foliage. Hardly surprising that horticulturists and garden specialists come here from all over the world. Even the determined non-gardener finds Ilnacullin a lovely place to visit: the views alone from its tree-fringed shoreline towards the Yellow Rocks, Garvillaun and Ship Island are worth it, and you often see seals sunbathing on the rocks as the ferry takes you to and fro. There is a Martello tower here too. George Bernard Shaw stayed on the island when working on his play, *St Joan*, in the early 1920s, although he freely admitted later that he hadn't finished it on his visit, doubtless distracted by the numerous opportunities for conversation. What writer hasn't preferred talking to actually applying pen to paper?

The boat ride back from Garinish/Ilnacullen gives quite a different view of Glengarriff and the surrounding shoreline. There are several expensive homes tucked discreetly into the trees around the bay, as well as older, decaying mansions, echoes of other days. Actress Maureen O'Hara was so taken with Glengarriff when she visited that she never left, and she wasn't the only one to lose her heart to this little bit of the Mediterranean set down in Ireland. Back on the pier, the little tin shed from which tickets were sold for the boat to Bantry still stands. Visitors came in their droves in one direction to admire the scenery, while reluctant emigrants, who knew from sad experience that beautiful scenery did not necessarily provide a living, went the other way, taking the *Lady Elsie* or the *Princess Beara* to Bantry, thence the train to Cork and on to Cobh.

Visitors still come to Glengarriff in great numbers, as the hotels, pubs, and shops selling knitwear and other souvenirs testify, but no longer by train and boat. Today they are more likely to take the twisting tunnel road from Kenmare, carved out of the living rock in the 1840s and probably the biggest single contributor to Glengarriff's development as a tourist centre. A little way up that

Opposite: Did Cromwell pass this way? Whether he did or not, the old arched bridge, now almost hidden beneath the luxuriant vegetation that characterises Glengarriff, still bears his name.

Kenmare road, Glengarriff Woods Nature Reserve is beautifully tucked away in a sheltered glen which stretches up along the Glengarriff river towards Barley Lake far above in the hills. It's one of those utterly peaceful places to ramble at any time of year, with venerable trees rustling above and the cheerful little stream ambling its way over sunlit gravel between mossy banks. The temptation to paddle or even take a dip in the clear, fresh mountain water is almost irresistible on a warm summer's day.

About the same distance out on the Castletownbere road, Cromwell's bridge is now bypassed twice over, but if you stop on the current bridge, walk on to the older bridge, and look upstream, you'll see its old stonework still arching gracefully over the river. Some say it was built during Cromwell's march west; others insist it had no link whatever with old Ironsides, but the name remains firmly established.

Towards Adrigole

Below: An oystercatcher comes gracefully to land, wings ready to fold away.

If you're in a hurry – although that's never a good idea in West Cork – take the main road for Adrigole. If, however, the day's your own, turn off left just after

Megannagan bridge and the Illaungarriff inlet on the narrower coastal route past Bocarnagh and Muccurragh to Tracashel and Coolieragh harbour. Here there is a whole cluster of tiny islets, each with its own unique name – Ilaunageragh, Carrigagour, Ilaunthieve, Coulagh. You can join the main road again just above Tracashel, but a few miles further on, turn off again at Derreenacarrin on a really pleasant wandering loop, which eventually gets right down to the water's edge and an old quay before turning west past Lough Naravy and Merchant's Lough. A side road beyond Derry Lough will take you down to Mehal Head, with a cave beneath the cliffs. And so up to Trafrask, with its memorial to five Sullivan brothers who served – and perished – together in the US Navy in World War II. They had asked not to be separated, and their wish was granted; but afterwards the rules were changed so that such a total loss within one family would not happen again. The quiet, pebbly strand and lapping waters of Trafrask, where their family originated, could hardly offer a greater contrast to the battleground of the South Pacific. The crew of the USS *Sullivans*, named for the brothers and their ultimate sacrifice, visited in 1964 to join in a special celebration honouring their memory.

Above: A ruined cottage at Trafrask. From just such a home must the ancestors of the O'Sullivan brothers have emigrated to America.

Beyond Trafrask, the first glimpses of Roancarrig lighthouse, on its lonely rock, come into view, and beyond that the rising bulk of Bere Island. Hungry Hill towers above the village of Adrigole, and if there has been recent rain (not an unusual occurrence), the Mare's Tail, Ireland's highest waterfall, comes cascading down the mountainside, much as the 'thousand wild fountains' fall from the cliffs encircling Gougane Barra after a downpour. Heading northwards into the hills from here is the Healy Pass, created as a project to give employment locally in the 1920s, and now offering a dramatic if demanding drive upwards in twists and turns to the Kerry border. At the summit stands a large Calvary, its blinding whiteness drawing the eye inexorably at every turn of the road.

Castletownbere and Bere Island

Castletownbere is the principal town of the Beara Peninsula as well as Ireland's leading whitefish port. Its fine natural harbour is effectively created by the sheltering length of Bere Island, which tempers the vagaries of the Atlantic beyond, and any day of the week the busy quays here make it obvious that this is very much a working town, with trawlers unloading their catch to be whisked

Opposite: The bulk of Hungry Hill dominates the skyline around Castletownbere.
Above: A rainbow arches over the impossibly-winding road up through the Healy Pass above Adrigole.

away in icy dignity to shops up country. Locals come down to buy their fish fresh from the sea too, and the restaurants are fortunate in being able to pick and choose a selection from the day's catch to cook that night. It's a good place to spend the evening, enjoying a seafood dinner and watching the hustle and bustle on the pier. Plenty of history to be discovered too, from ancient Brandy Hall bridge tucked away behind the Millbrook bar, to Dereenataggart Stone Circle up behind the Old Bakery.

Bere Island, only a mile from the mainland, but a world of its own, can be reached by two ferries: one from Pontoon, just before you reach Castletownbere, crosses to Lawrence Cove at the eastern end; the other, from the town quays, makes the shorter trip to a pier nearer to the western tip. At about 11km long by 5km wide, the island is pretty well the same size as Manhattan, but the population is somewhat less than that of the Big Apple – around two hundred year-round residents. That wasn't always the case: before the Famine, there were upwards of two thousand people living here, and those with a keen eye can discern the signs of that more crowded time in the remnants of old field systems and former habitations, now almost invisible underneath the bracken, gorse, and brambles. In fact, Bere Island has been inhabited for a very long time. A wedge

Left: Bere Island, looking up
towards Lawrence Cove.
Below: Wild flowers on a
country lane. Opposite:
Castletownbere is, above all, a
fishing port, as these brightly-
coloured trawlers testify.

tomb and hut site can be found at Ardaragh West, a promontory fort at Doonbeg, and a standing stone and circular enclosure at Greenane (a circular site is always clear evidence of Celtic presence, while square structures usually indicate Roman-influenced English). Later sites include Napoleonic towers and the remains of Victorian British military fortifications.

The O'Sullivan Beres owned the island until the power of the Gaelic chieftains was finally broken by the English in 1602. The island's first road also dates from this period – Sir George Carew ordered it to be built to transport the pro-English forces to the siege of Dunboy. Because of its highly strategic position at the mouth of Bantry Bay, Bere Island was always of considerable interest to the English government, who ensured it remained well guarded and fortified throughout their time in this country. Today, all strife forgotten, it's the most peaceful of places to visit and stay, with that wonderful sense of separation from the world's problems that islands always seem to give. The marina at Lawrence Cove is popular both with visiting yachts and the resident boating fraternity, offering, as it does, shelter from all but the most extreme weather conditions.

Dunboy

Dunboy is just beyond Castletownbere. Watch for a bend in the road and the old gates on the left, where the long driveway sweeps up along the shores of the bay. The original Dunboy Castle, a stronghold of the O'Sullivan Beres, now in ruins, stands at the very end of the promontory. Here its defenders fought against the English attackers to the last man, and all died. O'Sullivan Bere himself had managed to escape and made that march to Leitrim in the winter of 1603.

The rather grander mansion that comes into view on the right as you drive along the water's edge is Dunboy House, built by the copper magnates, the Puxleys, in the nineteenth century. Daphne du Maurier, a close friend of Christopher Puxley, recreated his ancestors and their world superbly in her 1943 novel *Hungry Hill*. It is tempting to imagine that she stayed here, but it is unlikely, since she would have been too young in its heyday. She probably heard a great many of the old family stories from Christopher, though. The house was burnt to the ground by the IRA in 1920 and lay in ruins for the rest of the twentieth century, its marble interiors and vaulted ceilings echoing only to the harsh croaks of ravens and the flutter of pigeons building above the elegant stonework of the windows. Today, it is in the lengthy process of being restored into an elegant hotel, so once again lights and music and fine dining may return to the old mansion. It is apparently

going to be called Dunboy Castle, but the old ruin may have something to say about that, perhaps even resurrecting a ghost or two to point out the error.

There is actually a little-known Victorian romantic thriller called *The Ghost of Dunboy Castle*, attributed to the pseudonymous 'Huberto'. It's clear, though, from the topographical detail, especially of the chapel standing next to the main building, that the author is basing his tale of terror in Dunboy House, the Puxleys' mansion, rather than the actual castle on the promontory. It suggests that he (or she) had at one time been a guest here. Or perhaps even one of the family, given the careful pseudonym. It's not a very good piece of literature, it has to be said, confused and rambling, but it has its entertaining moments:

> *Next to Dunboy Castle, though not part of the same building, was the private chapel of the O'Sullivans. It was possible to reach it, through a dark subterraneous passage, by lifting a flag in the centre of the hall, and descending an iron ladder … he heard the big clock strike, but scarcely noticed it. He then, with cautious step, descended the hard stone steps, and, putting the key in the door, unlocked it, and, drawing it towards him, laid open the vault. Then, to see his way, he directed the light of the lamp forward, when, lo ! a white form on the chair brought back the story Mrs. O'Brien had told him, and made a cold, creeping sensation pass over his entire frame. Then he saw those large eyes, widely open, staring at him, without a wink, without a motion. A supernatural awe overspread him, and fixed him to the ground, as, with tongue cleaving to his parched mouth, he muttered — "Oh, heavens ! her ghost ! her ghost!"*

While still on the Dunboy peninsula, you can take a small side road down past Cahergarriff to tiny Pulleen harbour, into which both Pulleen lakes (the main one and Little) empty themselves from the hills above. It's a peaceful little road, not much frequented apart from the occasional wandering sheep or cow, and you might see a seal floating in the bay beyond. The only way out is back again to the R572 leading ever westward. The coastal loop beckons again beyond Bealnagour, going round by Brackloon (there is a souterrain not far from here, on the coastal side of the road), and Lickbarrahane, before turning northwards again to join the main road at Knockroe bridge. Or you could take yet another road at this junction, which heads first to Black Ball Head, but then changes its mind and veers westward to White Ball Head with its promontory fort. After that it's again a question of retracing one's steps, but there are a couple of standing stones to anticipate, close to the main road by Knockroe bridge.

Dursey Island

A prominent wedge tomb in the field below the road marks the turn for Dursey, by Cloghfune, Firkeel Gap and Garinish before reaching Ballaghboy and the end of the road. Garinish (not to be confused with Garinish back in Glengarriff, nor yet that nearer Kenmare; the name means 'the near island' so there are several), lashed on windy days by the thundering waves, must surely hold one of the most remote post offices in the land. But not a whit discouraged by the salt spray, the doughty postman here takes the mail even further. Dursey is the only place in Ireland where the letters arrive by cable car. As do visitors, newspapers, the occasional cow, and a supply of slates for somebody's roof.

Ireland's only cable car was installed in 1969. Before that, islanders had to rely on light rowboats to get them across the dangerous Dursey Sound to the mainland. Recently, when the old cabin had to be replaced, along with one of the steel cables, residents had to return to the sea trip for several months before the service was up and running again. Sheepdogs travel regularly in the cable car, keeping a sharp eye on their woolly flock who also cross by this method; they don't carry individual season tickets, but know perfectly well when to leap on and off. It's not unusual to share the swinging cabin with dog, ewes, glass for a broken window, foodstuffs, and of course the postman with his bag of letters.

Its Irish name, Inis Baoi, refers to the Hag of Beara, a female figure of great power in Celtic lore, and one we will encounter again further up the peninsula. Traders of old navigated by Dursey as they hugged the coastline, avoiding the open sea. Vikings called it Thjorsey, or 'The Bull Island' – a name still commemorated in the Bull Rock which stands adjacent, bearing a vital lighthouse. Legend has it that these fierce raiders held captured slaves on Dursey before shipping them to far-off lands to be sold. Monks built a monastery here in medieval times, and you can still see its ruins today. The Great O'Sullivan Bere was born on Dursey; and throughout the island's history there are many stirring tales of shipwrecks, sieges, tragedy and courage. A signal tower erected here during the Napoleonic wars was part of a chain of warning beacons stretching right around Ireland. Northwards, the legendary Skelligs, off the Kerry coast, can be seen, once home to communities of monks who sought those precipitous and unwelcoming rocks in pursuit of holiness and peace.

Because it is sited in such a westerly position off the edge of the Irish coast, Dursey is often the first landfall for American birds blown off course, and over the years it has notched up an impressive number of rarities. Scanning with binoculars might well reveal dolphins or whales making their way past the island too. The strong Atlantic winds discourage most plants from growing too tall, but one exception is the tree mallow, which can soar to over two metres in sheltered spots. Heather and gorse cover the uplands with a haze of purple and gold, and lichens, once used for dyeing purposes, colour the rocks on the shoreline. Peacock butterflies alight on blue sheep's-bit scabious, and the striped caterpillars of the cinnabar moth feed on yellow ragwort, while pink cushions of stonecrop thrive on the undulating stone walls.

Of course, like every self-respecting island, Dursey has its share of legends. Ghostly fishing boats have been seen by fishermen returning after dark; such apparitions usually foretell storms. Strange lights on shore at night appear to follow boatmen as they move along under the cliffs to set their lobster pots. Odd noises are heard by householders downstairs in the wee small hours, but nothing

Dursey Island stretches out into the Atlantic, a navigation point for sailors from ancient times.

is found disturbed the following morning. And, of course, on an island where piracy and shipwreck were frequent occurrences, there are many tales of buried treasure lying hidden, waiting for the lucky finder.

Allihies

Turning back eastwards from Dursey, steps must be retraced until you reach that wedge tomb at the junction with the main road again; although determined hikers can follow the north coast along the slopes of Lackacrogan, Foher and Dooneen Point. Soon, brightly-coloured Allihies comes into view, its many-hued houses spreading out along the bay underneath the sheltering hills. In fact, the correct name of the village is Cluin, but everybody has got into the habit of calling it Allihies (from *na h'ailichi*, or 'the cliff fields'), after the surrounding parish. Here you are surrounded by copper-mining history. The hills are literally honeycombed with shafts, passageways, chasms, pits, vast subterranean workings.

It is definitely dangerous to go too close, or even to consider the insane idea of exploring, but to climb a breezy hillside (keeping a secure grip of children and dogs) and look from behind the safety of wire fencing at the vast dark caverns opening in the ground below you, their sides gleaming with the iridescent coppery green that marks the presence of the valuable ore, is an unforgettable experience.

Copper, and copper mining, have been part of life here right back to the Bronze Age, as archaeological digs have shown. The most productive period however was in the nineteenth century, when, with the Puxley family of Dunboy in charge, almost 300,000 tons of ore was shipped out of West Cork. At its height, it employed some 1,500 men who lived with their families all over this area. When the price of copper plummeted in the 1880s, due to large-scale discoveries of the ore in South America, the region saw huge emigration, much of it to Butte, Montana, where families still trace their line back to West Cork. Today, Allihies has a tiny population, and the silence is unbroken over the boulder-strewn hillsides which once echoed to the noise of industry.

Prominent above the village is the mountain mine man-engine house, installed in 1862 to bring the workers from the daylight skies into the black depths (as frighteningly deep as 460 metres or so – 1,500 feet) each day, and back to the surface again at the end of their shift. Not only unique in Ireland, it is the sole remaining purpose-built man-engine house anywhere in the world, and as such has recently been conserved by the Mining Heritage Trust of Ireland.

There is an interesting Copper Mining Museum in the village, housed in a chapel built by Cornish miners in 1845. With great foresight, someone has created a café here too, and when you've climbed the hillsides, seen the mineshafts, and learned some of the region's history in the museum displays, you can enjoy home baking and look out at the sunlit stretches of Ballydonegan beach, its very sand created from particles washed down from the mines above.

And so on to Eyeries, another brightly-painted village. The TV series based on Deirdre Purcell's acclaimed novel, *Falling for a Dancer*, was filmed largely in and around Eyeries, as was the earlier 1977 film, *Purple Taxi*. There are more standing stones, stone circles, stone rows and tombs in the vicinity than you could shake a stick at, as well as the Ballycrovane Ogham Stone, while down on the shore past Eyeriesbegga, where the Caol Inse river enters the sea, Pallas strand is a reminder of the old days when 'fish palaces' were set up to salt the then-plentiful pilchard and herring in so many places around the West Cork coast. The R571 heads up from here over the Slieve Miskish range towards Castletownbere; but a few miles up, turning off left at Kealincha bridge will bring you into another wildly beautiful region full of the same stone monuments to a lost past. A splendidly tall standing stone, a full 3m high, can be found at Kilmackowen on the hillside here, close to a megalithic tomb. With the wind sweeping over the heather and the clouds changing the light from sunshine to gloom and back again in a few seconds, it's not hard to imagine the sound of ancient voices and the tread of feet long gone.

About half way to Ardgroom, a westward turn leads to the Kilcatherine peninsula. Past the turn for Lough Fadda are the ruins of Kilcatherine church and graveyard, a place so old that not even the experts are entirely sure what date to put on it. It is, however, believed to have been built by the same monks who created the beehive monastery on Skellig Michael. The thing to look for here, above all else, is the strange cat's face on a carved stone above a doorway. Similar carvings have been discovered in Austria and Italy and it may well be pre-Christian in origin, like the Sheela-na-gigs or fertility goddesses found elsewhere in Ireland.

That's entirely in keeping for the Kilcatherine peninsula, since a little further on, at the top of a hill overlooking Coulagh – or Cailleach – Bay, stands the legendary great grey rock, An Cailleach Beara. The Hag of Beara is a key matriarchal figure of ancient Irish beliefs, a mother goddess in her third

manifestation, the Crone. It is not known when exactly the rock itself became linked to the goddess of old, but it has, naturally enough, gathered many legends and beliefs over the centuries. There is an old Irish saying, 'The age of the yew, the age of the eagle, and the age of the Cailleach Beara', and indeed the Hag is held to have lived seven lifetimes before being turned to stone. Now she waits, immovable, for her true husband, Manannán MacLir, god of the sea, to return to her.

She is also the narrator of a tenth-century Irish poem, 'The Lament of the Old Woman of Beare'. It is never a simple matter to translate a poem from one language to another, particularly the decorative, word-rich style of old Irish to the more restrained format of English. There is so much that is understood, taken as read in one language that is entirely lost in the new. Dr Kuno Meyer's 1913 rendering took the view that this was simply an aged 'good-time girl' mourning for happy times past, but Lady Gregory's 1919 translation, though less smooth and poetic in layout, perhaps came closer to reflecting the lament for an ancient pre-Christian Ireland irrevocably lost:

It is of Corca Dubhne she was, and she had her youth seven times over, and every man that had lived with her died of old age, and her grandsons and great-grandsons were tribes and races. And through a hundred years she wore upon her head the veil Cuimire had blessed. Then age and weakness came upon her and it is what she said:

Ebb-tide to me as to the sea; old age brings me reproach; I used to wear a shift that was always new; to-day, I have not even a cast one.

It is riches you are loving, it is not men; it was men we loved in the time we were living.

There were dear men on whose plains we used to be driving; it is good the time we passed with them; it is little we were broken afterwards.

When my arms are seen it is long and thin they are; once they used to be fondling, they used to be around great kings…
(The Kiltartan Poetry Book, 1919)

Coins, pebbles, trinkets and other small offerings placed on and around the rock are evidence that even the most modern-minded tourist will still instinctively revert to the old ways of showing respect, even if the reasons are not fully comprehended.

The road continues around the Kilcatherine peninsula by Derryvegan Lough, Cleanderry harbour, and evidence of another former fishing industry in Pallas harbour by Dog's Nose Point, before curving round the sweep of Ardgroom harbour into the village of the same name, by Cappul or Horse bridge. Here you are very close to the Kerry border, but there are still more hidden treasures to be discovered in West Cork. Right across the main road is a side track leading up to beautiful Glenbeg Lough, deep in the mountains. The young Rudyard Kipling went fishing here when his ship anchored in Berehaven in 1898:

The animal delight of that roaring day of sun and wind will live long in our memory. We had it all to ourselves – the rifted purple flank of Lackawee, the long vista of the lough darkening as the shadows fell; the smell of a new country, and the tearing wind that brought down mysterious voices of men from somewhere high above us.
[A Fleet in Being, 1898]

Between Ardgroom and the boundary with Kerry, hardly 4km, there are no fewer than five laneways all leading up into the hills, like that to Glenbeg.

Between them they offer a total of two stone circles, one stone row, a standing stone, several cairns, and finally a boulder burial, just before the border – a most satisfactory way to end the tour. Or you could, of course, continue on to Lauragh in Kerry, take the Healy Pass back to Adrigole (the view of Glenmore Lake far below is heartstopping) and start all over again. You'll find different things every time.

Best of all, perhaps, try to time your day so that you can be on the slopes of Slieve Miskish above Allihies as the sun sets. The vista that opens up as sea and sky turn to a dazzling gold, and the coastline is etched in black, is one you will carry with you forever.

Opposite: The strange and unique stone carving of a cat's face on the old church at Kilcatherine. **Below:** An old ring fort near Ardgroom.

Looking back from the slopes above Allihies towards Dursey at sunset.

MAPS

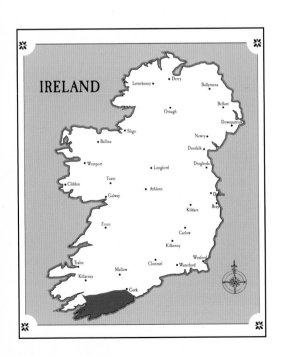

IRELAND

CHAPTER 1: TRUE WEST
Gearagh, Gaeltacht, Gougane

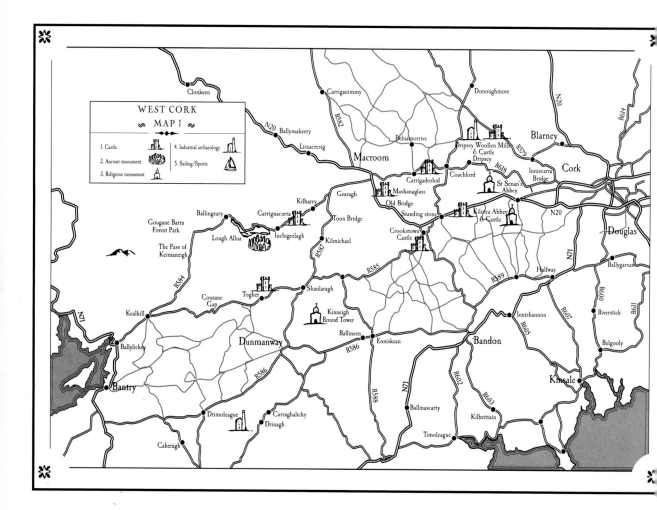

CHAPTER II: THE ROAD WINDS WEST
Old Head, Baltimore, the Islands

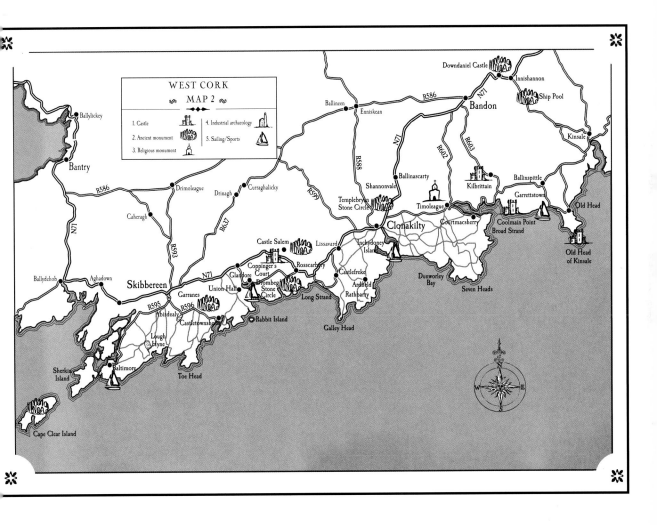

WEST CORK
≈ MAP 2 ≈

1. Castle
2. Ancient monument
3. Religious monument
4. Industrial archaeology
5. Sailing/Sports

Ballylickey

Bantry

Ballineen
Enniskean
R586
N71
Bandon
Downdaniel Castle
Innishannon
Ship Pool
Kinsale

Drimoleague
Drinagh
Curraghalicky
R599
R588
R602
R603
Ballinascarty
Kilbrittain
Ballinspittle
Old Head

Caheragh
R637
Shannonvale
Templebryan
Stone Circle
Timoleague
Garrettstown
Coolmain Point
Broad Strand
Old Head
of Kinsale

N71
R593
Clonakilty
Courtmacsherry

Ballydehob
Aghadown
Skibbereen
N71
Castle Salem
Coppinger's
Court
Lissavard
Rosscarbery
Inchydoney
Island
Castlefreke
Dunworley
Bay
Seven Heads

Garranes
Glandore
Union Hall
Drombeg
Stone
Circle
Ardfield
Rathbarry
Long Strand

R595
R596
Abbeydealy
Castletownshend
Rabbit Island
Galley Head

Lough
Hyne

Sherkin
Island
Baltimore
Toe Head

Cape Clear Island

W E

CHAPTER III: OF SMUGGLERS AND SHIPWRECKS

The Mizen Peninsula

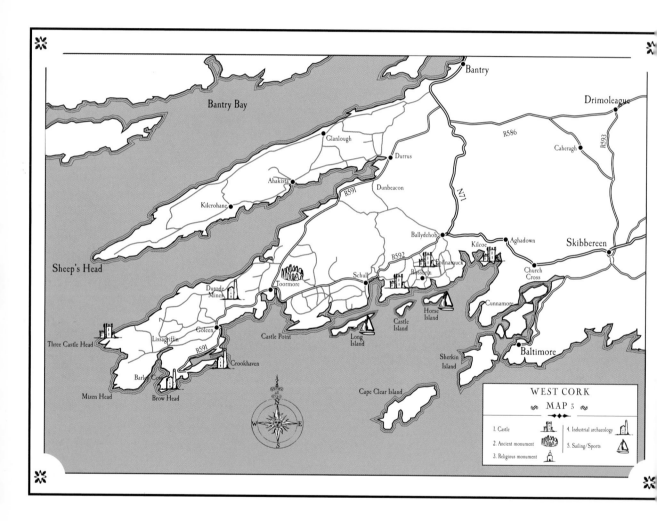

CHAPTER IV: AT THE WORLD'S END

The Beara Peninsula

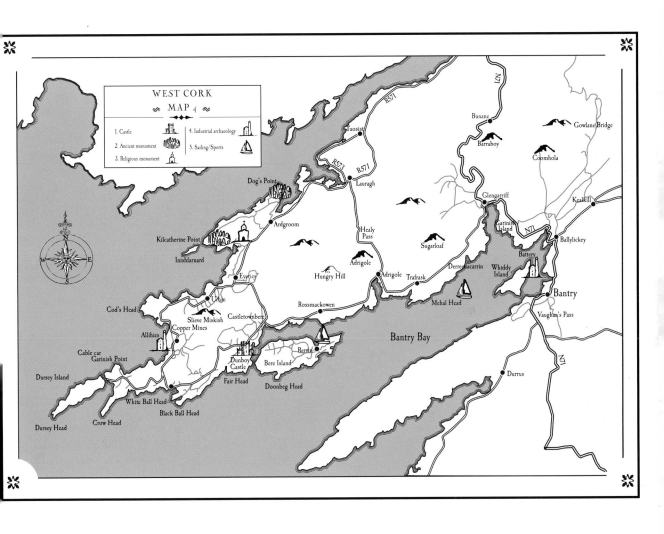

WEST CORK

MAP 4

1. Castle
2. Ancient monument
3. Religious monument
4. Industrial archaeology
5. Sailing/Sports

Tuosist

Bunane

Gowlane Bridge

Barraboy

Coomhola

R571

R573

R571

Dog's Point

Lauragh

Glengarriff

Kealkill

Ardgroom

Healy Pass

Garinish Island

N71

Ballylickey

Kilcatherine Point

Sugarloaf

Battery

Inishfarnard

Adrigole

Derreenacarrin

Whiddy Island

Eyeries

Hungry Hill

Adrigole

Trafrask

Bantry

Urhin

Rossmackowen

Mehal Head

Cod's Head

Slieve Miskish
Copper Mines

Castletownbere

Vaughan's Pass

Allihies

Bantry Bay

N71

Cable car
Garinish Point

Dunboy Castle

Rerrin

Bere Island

Durrus

Dursey Island

Fair Head

Doonbeg Head

White Ball Head

Black Ball Head

Dursey Head

Crow Head

INDEX

(*Numbers in Italics indicate illustrations*)

Page 152: Foxgloves on a
footpath at Gougane Barra.
Page 158: Choughs – West
Cork is one of their remaining
strongholds in Europe.
Page 160: Fuchsia, the
characteristic flower of
West Cork.